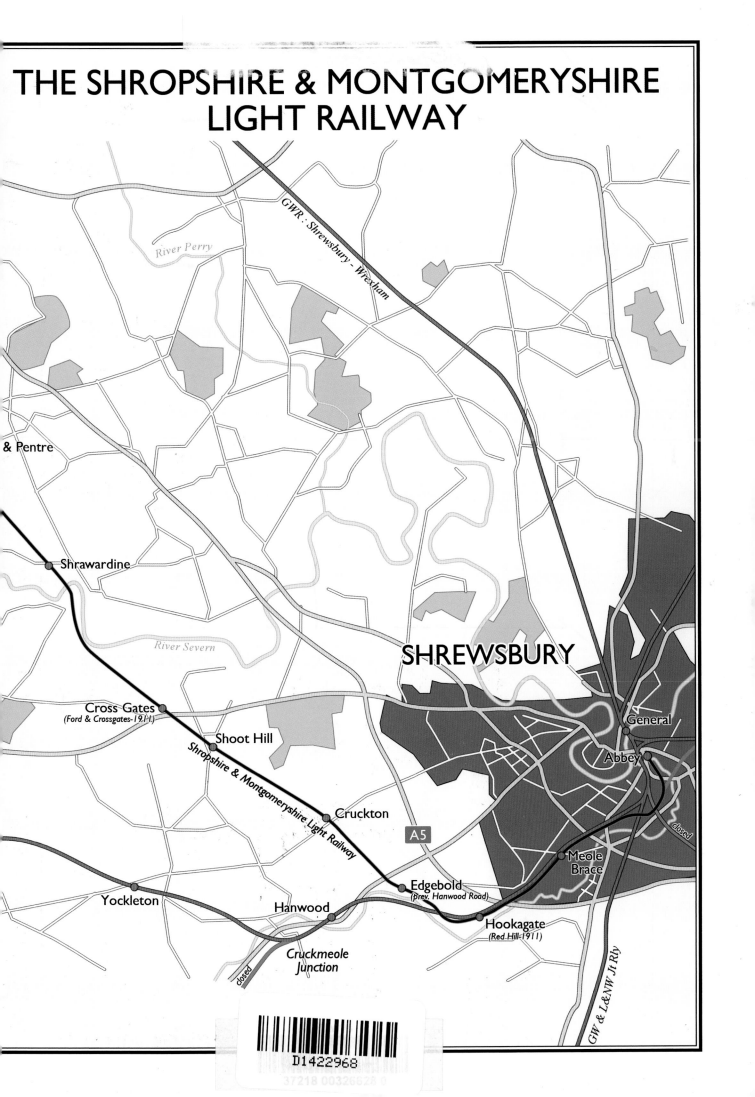

THE SHROPSHIRE & MONTGOMERYSHIRE LIGHT RAILWAY

GWR : Shrewsbury - Wrexham

River Perry

& Pentre

Shrawardine

River Severn

SHREWSBURY

Cross Gates
(Ford & Crossgates-1911)

Shoot Hill

Shropshire & Montgomeryshire Light Railway

Cruckton

A5

General

Abbey

closed

Meole
Brace

Yockleton

Hanwood

Edgebold
(prev. Hanwood Road)

Hookagate
(Red.Hill-1911)

closed

Cruckmeole
Junction

GW & L&NW Jt Rly

An Illustrated History of the

Shropshire and Montgomeryshire Light Railway

An
Illustrated History
of the
Shropshire and Montgomeryshire Light Railway

Peter Johnson

An imprint of
Ian Allan Publishing

First published 2008

ISBN 978 0 86093 619 0

© Peter Johnson 2008

Published by Oxford Publishing Co

an imprint of Ian Allan Publishing Ltd, Hersham, Surrey KT12 4RG.
Printed in England by Ian Allan Printing Ltd, Hersham, Surrey KT12 4RG.

Code: 0807/B1

Visit the Ian Allan Publishing website at www.ianallanpublishing.com

Front cover: **One of the two locomotives supplied new to the Shropshire & Montgomeryshire Light Railway, Hawthorn, Leslie 0-6-2T *Thisbe* posed with its crew at Llanymynech.** *Author's collection*

Back cover (top): **Manning, Wardle 0-6-0ST *Morous* and Dodman 2-2-2WT *Gazelle* at Kinnerley on 19 May 1911.** *T. R. Perkins collection*

Back cover (bottom): **Extract from a plan deposited by the Shrewsbury & Potteries Junction Railway in 1865.** *HLRO*

Endpapers: **Map of the Shropshire & Montgomeryshire Light Railway.** *Gordon Rushton*

The Shropshire & Montgomeryshire Light Railway has been fighting a valiant but losing battle for many years, and although the scars of the early occupation were partly healed by the present occupiers this last engagement was decisive and it is sad to think that its demise will be without medals.

John L. Bullock
Commercial Office,
British Railways (Western Region)
26 February 1960

Half title page: **SMLR ex-LSWR 0-6-0 No 3 *Hesperus*, no longer in the prime of condition, receives attention while standing at Shrewsbury with the ex-Midland Railway passenger brake van.** *A. M. Davies collection*

Title page: **When the War Office had control of the SMLR new sidings and locomotive servicing facilities were installed at Hookagate. Ex-LNWR 0-6-0 No 8182 stands at the water tower in June 1947.** *Michael Whitehouse collection*

Below: **A pair of BR Class 25s pass the rail-welding depot at Hookagate with the Aberystwyth–Euston working on 31 July 1976. The depot was built on the site of the WD exchange sidings after the SMLR had been closed.** *Andrew Bannister*

Contents

Introduction

Today, the Shropshire & Montgomeryshire Light Railway is largely known for the involvement of the light railway engineer and entrepreneur Colonel Stephens, and the eclectic collections of locomotives and rolling stock with which he equipped it. Over the years, some £2 million capital was spent on this rural railway but most of the investors saw nothing for their investment. In the annals of British railway history the SMLR's story must rank as one of heroic and misguided failure.

The railway, a main line and branches totalling 30 miles, served an area on the Welsh border to the west of Shrewsbury, intersected by the River Severn, which was predominantly agricultural with two stone-quarrying centres, a small local population, and surrounded by existing railways.

Its tale is one of legal disputes, financiers, bankruptcy, abandonment, aged locomotives and rolling stock, failure to complete authorised lines, several changes of name, a closure on the orders of the Board of Trade, numerous Acts of Parliament and, most successfully, a period of operation by the military.

The SMLR itself was opened in 1911 but it has its origins in the 'railway mania' of the 1860s. Legal activity started in 1862 and by the time the Potteries, Shrewsbury & North Wales Railway (PSNWR) was opened in 1866, a further eight acts had been obtained for new lines, deviations, additional funding, and extensions of time. What had started as the West Shropshire Mineral Railway, intending to connect Llanymynech, on the Oswestry & Newtown Railway, with Shrewsbury, via a connection to the Shrewsbury & Welshpool Railway near Westbury, was first the Shrewsbury & North Wales Railway but then became, by amalgamation with the Shrewsbury & Potteries Junction Railway, a route to Market Drayton, the PSNWR.

Consisting of a line from Shrewsbury to Llanymynech with mineral branches to Criggion and Llanyblodwel, the railway had consumed £1.3 million capital for 28 miles of route, making it the most expensive non-metropolitan railway in the country. Much futile effort expended on the eastwards connection to Market Drayton was not abandoned until 1918. West of Shrewsbury, proposed extensions would have served Llangynog in the Tanat Valley, Breidden, Nesscliffe, Criggion, Llanfair Caereinion and Llanyblodwell; tramways would have served Nantmawr and Moat Hall.

The PSNWR's development was under the control of Richard Samuel France who worked as a contractor and financier and leased quarries at Criggion and Nantmawr. He borrowed money to fund the construction and was bankrupted following the collapse of the discount house Overend, Gurney & Co in May 1866. The aftermath had the PSNWR in receivership and the line closed before the year's end.

It was to be another two years before a financial reconstruction enabled the railway to be re-opened, but it was not a success and another receiver was appointed in 1873. By 1880, the railway was not only in serious debt, but was badly run down. Following a complaint by a member of the public it was closed on the orders of the Board of Trade, to be abandoned, although not quite neglected, for nearly 30 years. The Cambrian Railways took over responsibility for the Nantmawr branch and this section became the only part of the PSNWR to have any amount of consistent traffic.

An attempt to revive the remainder of the PSNWR came in 1888, with another Act of Parliament and a new name, Shropshire Railways. Despite renewing some of the track and bringing the capital expended on it to nearly £2 million this company failed even to reopen the railway, leaving it to nature once again. Its bondholders benefited from the Nantmawr branch rent until the company was nationalised in 1948.

The SR was not forgotten, however, and deliverance came in 1909, when the infamous Holman Fred Stephens devised a scheme to lease and reconstruct the railway and to operate it under the auspices of the 1896 Light Railways Act. Equipped with a diverse and increasingly ramshackle collection of rolling stock, the SMLR managed to keep going, notwithstanding the withdrawal of passenger services in 1933, until the Second World War, when the Ministry of Transport and the War Office prevented it from fading away entirely.

Brought under government control on the outbreak of war, a substantial part of the SMLR was then proposed for abandonment when the War Office decided that it was ideally located to supply an ammunition depot it wished to develop in the area. As a result the railway, apart from the Criggion branch, was relaid and continued in use until 1960. So, the railway that had first been opened in 1866 justified its existence for just two decades. Except for the extremities at Nantmawr and Shrewsbury Abbey, which remained in use for a few years longer, the track was being lifted barely 100 years after the whole venture started.

In the final analysis the SMLR should not have been built, and it was more by luck than judgement that it lasted as long as it did. In the first instance a proper examination of traffic prospects should have produced just short branches to serve the Nantmawr and Criggion quarries. As it was, France's flawed ambition to develop a network resulted in a railway with little potential traffic and the wastage of vast sums of money. Sir Richard Green Price Bt took on the Shropshire Railways with enthusiasm but was hampered by a shortage of funds and a willingness to litigate rather than mediate. Where Price failed, Holman Fred Stephens apparently succeeded. The railway was rebuilt and reopened but its veneer of success, payment of dividends and debenture interest, was a sham dependent on capital expenditure made from revenue not being depreciated, and on creditors not chasing for payment. Without the war the SMLR would have been closed as soon as any of the creditors refused to allow further credit. The likelihood is that the railway would have been abandoned once again, for want of sufficient assets to justify receivership and liquidation. In the end, the War Office was the railway's saviour, giving it nearly 20 years of worthwhile existence.

Remarkably, as this book is being written, a small part of the PSNWR still lies abandoned, with rails in place albeit barely visible in the undergrowth, and is the subject of a scheme to revive it. The Nantmawr branch was the only success of France's Shropshire ambitions, part of it remaining in use for its original purpose, the transport of stone, until 1971. Nowadays, only the *cognoscenti* know where the PSNWR's successor, the Shropshire & Montgomeryshire Light Railway, used to pass but it is not ignored. Its complex and chequered history, together with the involvement of Colonel Stephens, combine to keep its memory alive where other similar lines have long been forgotten.

Acknowledgements

Thomas Richard Perkins, a chemist from Henley-in-Arden, was the first to write about the Shropshire & Montgomeryshire Light Railway and its background from a historical perspective, with articles published in *The Railway Magazine*. Accompanied by his brother G. M. Perkins and their friend F. E. Fox-Davies, a grocer in Llanymynech, he explored the derelict PSNWR/SR while his companions photographed it. Without their efforts the photographic record of the abandoned railway would be considerably poorer. With the creation of the SMLR they maintained their interest; Perkins and Fox-Davies saw or travelled on the first train on 13 April 1911 and in 1921 Perkins had a free first class pass for 'all stations' on the SMLR, signed by, but not issued by, Colonel Stephens. After his death in 1952, Perkins' collection came into the ownership of W. E. Hayward and is now available to view, with much other material, as a part of the WEH-LYN Collection at the National Archives at Kew.

At the National Archives I also examined records created by the Board of Trade, the Ministry of Transport, the War Office, Companies House, and the Cambrian Railways. Records deposited there by the former British Railways Records Office include the minute books of the Shropshire Railways and the SMLR and SR's stock and transfer registers. I have also seen the records and plans relating to the numerous acts engendered by this railway at the House of Lords Records Office. The availability of these organisations' catalogues on-line has been a great help. The *London Gazette*, also available on-line, was of use in determining the progress of legislation and the military career of Colonel Stephens. Most of the Board of Trade returns were studied at the University of Leicester Library.

In no particular order I am particularly indebted to John Keylock, Michael Davies, Alan Donaldson, Vic Bradley, Adrian Gray, Hugh Ballantyne, Michael Whitehouse, Mike Hart, Vic Mitchell, Peter Jarvis, Pat and Geoff Ward, Brian Janes, Chris Milner, Ian Bendall, Jane Kennedy and Ian Kennedy for providing assistance, support and/or the loan of material or information. Special thanks are due to Gordon Rushton for providing the endpapers and redrawing the track layouts. The core data contained within Appendix 1 has been extracted from the publications of the Industrial Railway Society and I thank the society's chairman for permission to use it; it has been amended in the light of information encountered in primary sources.

For myself, I have had a fascinating journey trawling through over 100 years of documents to try to work out how the West Shropshire Mineral Railway became the SMLR via the Potteries, Shrewsbury & North Wales Railway and the Shropshire Railways at a cost of some £2 million. And I still don't know where all the money went! It remains to say that I accept responsibility for any errors.

Peter Johnson
Leicester
March 2008

Abbreviations

BoT	Board of Trade
BS	Brown, Shipley & Co
BTC	British Transport Commission
CSdL	Cutbill, Son & de Lungo
EKLR	East Kent Light Railway
GWR	Great Western Railway
KESLR	Kent & East Sussex Light Railway
LNWR	London & North Western Railway
LSWR	London & South Western Railway
LRO	Light Railway Order
ONR	Oswestry & Newtown Railway
PSNWR	Potteries, Shrewsbury & North Wales Railway
SMLR	Shropshire & Montgomeryshire Light Railway
SNWR	Shrewsbury & North Wales Railway
SPJR	Shrewsbury & Potteries Junction Railway
SR	Shropshire Railways
SWR	Shrewsbury & Welshpool Railway
TVLR	Tanat Valley Light Railway
WD	War Department
WO	War Office
WSMR	West Shropshire Mineral Railway

Conventions

An omission from a quoted document is indicated by an ellipsis (...) and an editorial insertion by the use of square brackets ([]).

During the period covered
£1 = 240d (pence) = 20s (shillings); 1s = 12d;
    £1 guinea = £1 1s.
1 ton = 20 hundredweight (cwt); 1cwt = 4 quarters (qtr);
    1qtr = 2 stone (st); 1st = 14 pounds (lb);
    1lb = 16 ounces (oz)
1 mile = 8 furlongs = 80 chains = 1,760 yards;
    1 chain = 22 yards

The value of money

Equivalent value of £1 in 2007

1860	£43.16	1920	£21.21
1870	£45.70	1925	£29.97
1880	£48.31	1930	£33.42
1890	£49.89	1935	£36.98
1900	£57.06	1940	£28.72
1905	£57.35	1945	£25.95
1910	£57.06	1950	£22.78
1915	£43.06		

Data extracted from the currency converter on the National Archives website: www.nationalarchives.gov.uk/currency/

Setting the scene – the mania and afterwards

The area to the west of Shrewsbury reaching to the Welsh border is largely lush agricultural land that benefits from being a flood plain of the River Severn and its tributaries. Within this area is a triangle of land bordered by three roads: along its eastern side is Telford's Holyhead road, the A5, which reaches an apex with the Oswestry to Newtown road, the A483, near the former, and is completed by the Welshpool to Shrewsbury road, the A458. To the west of the triangle are outcrops of limestone that reach 700ft above sea level at Llanymynech and Nantmawr, and 900ft at Criggion. The earliest signs of quarrying, for copper, lead and zinc at Llanymynech, have been dated to 200BC. Nantmawr produced aggregates, its stone considered to be of high quality,

but is now classified as dormant. In the past Criggion produced cobbles and roadstone but now, the only active quarry of the three, it produces aggregates which are transported by road. Used for both grazing and arable farming in the 19th century, much of the property was tenanted, being in the estates of either the Earl of Bradford or the Earl of Powis.

Habitation consists of hamlets and small villages, the largest communities being established at Kinnerley and Llanymynech, with around 1,000 souls, the latter set astride the English-Welsh border. Shrewsbury itself, located strategically on the Severn, is a substantial market town that has trebled in size from the 31,280 residents recorded in the 1801 census.

Prior to the development of the railways the most significant transport links in the area were Telford's road, running north-west from Shrewsbury, and to the west, the Montgomery Canal, a route that was particularly advantageous for the stone quarries, and later a part of the Shropshire Union system.

By 1865 the area was surrounded by railways: the Shrewsbury & Chester Railway from 1848, running north–south to the east; the Oswestry & Newtown Railway (ONR) along the western flank from 1860, and part of the Cambrian Railways from 1864, and, completing the triangle, the Shrewsbury & Welshpool Railway (SWR) from east to west which was to the south, and opened in 1862. A branch of the

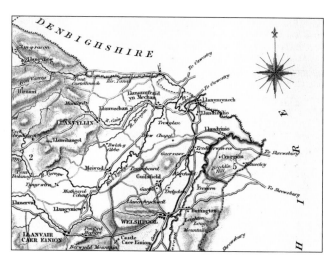

Left: **Montgomeryshire location map, 1840.** *R. Creighton, Lewis's Topographical Dictionary, extract/Author's collection*

Below: **Shropshire location map, 1840.** *R. Creighton, Lewis's Topographical Dictionary, extract/Author's collection*

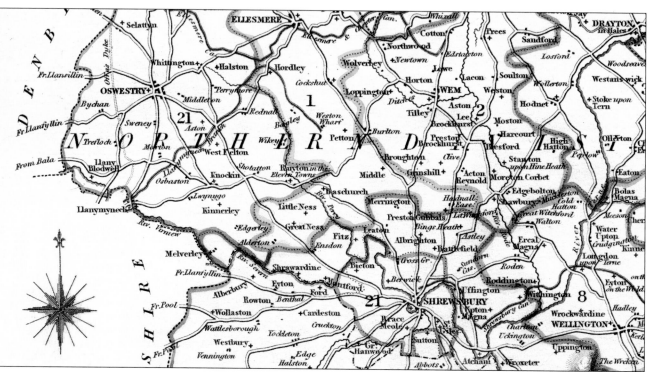

ONR served the quarries at Porthywaen from Llynclys, slightly beyond the area covered by this book but close to Nantmawr. The lines that radiated out from Shrewsbury were all controlled by the Great Western Railway or the London & North Western Railway, either separately or jointly, those large companies having an agreement that neither would undertake any expansion in the area without the support of the other.

Two proposals to cross the triangle by rail had been submitted to Parliament in 1861. That of the West Midland, Shrewsbury & Coast of Wales Railway was intended to be a trunk route for traffic to and from Ireland, the proposed route from Shrewsbury being via Kinnerley to Llanyblodwel and into the Tanat Valley. This was substantially the route taken by the Potteries, Shrewsbury & North Wales Railway at a later date. The level of opposition from the Oswestry & Newtown Railway and the residents of Llanfyllin, angry at being bypassed, was sufficient for the bill to be rejected in Parliament.

The West Shropshire Mineral Railway (WSMR) act gained royal assent on 29 July 1862. It contained powers for the construction of a railway from the ONR near Llanymynech to the SWR near Yockleton, about 12 miles, with a bridge over the Severn near Shrawardine to be opened to both road and rail users. The promoters were William Walter Cargill, Richard Augustus Bethell, Arthur Pittar Lattey, Elias Mocatta and Charles Pool Froom, who became the first directors. The company seal featured a primitive illustration of an early 2-2-2, but the company was not to acquire any locomotives.

The motive for developing the railway is unclear as unlike many such schemes it did not appear to arise from a local demand for access to an obvious trading centre. In this case Richard Samuel France seemed to be the guiding light. He was involved with several railway promotions in the West Midlands and Wales. Initially an employee of the Mid Wales Railway and then the SWR, he started acting as promoter, financier and contractor on his own account. It was often the practice of contractors to take shares in lieu of payment, with the intention of selling them at a profit when the railway was completed, or in anticipation that the completed railway would be sold to a larger company, as had been the case with the SWR, built independently and then sold to the London & North Western Railway. At different times, France was described as a railway contractor, a quarry owner, and a colliery owner. He leased the 25 acres of quarries at Criggion for 21 years from 1864, and at Nantmawr, almost certainly with the intention of delivering traffic to the railway and to increase his influence on it.

Although France was not named as a promoter in the act he was identified as such in an agreement that he made with the LNWR on 12 June 1862. Having initially objected to the bill the LNWR withdrew its objection on receiving France's undertaking that the WSMR would not build proposed branches from the SWR and the Severn Valley Railway to Shrewsbury General station, would withdraw its application for running powers over the SWR, would grant the LNWR running powers over the WSMR, and would not compete with the LNWR or the SWR.

As incorporated, the WSMR could raise share capital of £90,000 and borrow up to £30,000 subject to conditions. Level crossings were permitted at Kinnerley and Shrawardine. Three years were allowed to exercise compulsory purchase powers with five years allowed for the completion of construction. The rates for the carriage of various classifications of goods were specified as were, notwithstanding the railway's title, rates for the carriage of passengers. Perhaps the company was not intending to work all trains itself, or indeed any, as it was empowered to charge for 'the use of engines for propelling

West Shropshire Mineral Railway Company seal. *National Archives*

carriages'. The use of the word 'carriages' in this context was a portmanteau word to refer to any vehicle used on the railway. Three classes of passengers were allowed for. The ONR could make use of the railway with its own 'engines, carriages and wagons', the act containing no reference to the LNWR.

The two branch lines that the WSMR had wished to make in Shrewsbury and the SWR's running powers would have been of considerable advantage to it, by reducing haulage costs on through traffic. In trying to find a solution, it deposited another bill, seeking fresh powers in November.

In the meantime, another act of 1862 had a significant effect on future events relating to the WSMR and its development. The Limited Liability Act was the third of a series intended to encourage enterprise whilst limiting the personal liability of company members. This was not applicable to railway companies created by statute but it did create a boom in promotions of all sorts and by 1866 more than 3,000 companies had been registered. A consequence of this was that some of the new companies were lending money to ventures that were ill-conceived.

The WSMR's 1863 act approved a deviation from Shrawardine to Red Hill, near Meole Brace on the outskirts of Shrewsbury. This increased the length of the WSMR to 15 miles from 12, but also had the benefit of reducing the overall distance by one mile, with the replaced section formally abandoned. The ONR's use of the line was continued and the conditions for constructing a junction with the SWR specified. Up to £60,000 capital could be raised by issuing shares and £20,000 by mortgage. Four years were allowed for construction, including three for the use of the compulsory purchase powers. Traffic agreements were permitted to be made between the WSMR and the LNWR, the GWR, the West Midland Railway, the SWR and the ONR, or any of them.

The act also permitted the WSMR to strike off, literally, in a new direction, to the Shropshire coalfield. From the junction with SWR a short line, called the Moat Hall Tramway on the plans or the Moat Hall Railway in the act, was authorised to branch off to the south-west in a trailing direction. Part of the route would have run alongside the road, terminating near Annscroft. If the company chose to use horses, haulage could be charged for at the same rate as if locomotives were used.

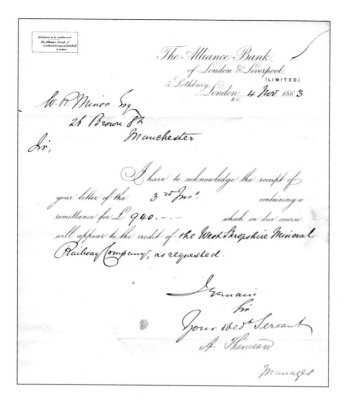

Bank receipt for £940 to be invested in the West Shropshire Mineral Railway, 1863. *Author's collection*

The railway's plans for a line from Llanymynech to Llangynog, in the Tanat Valley, a tramway to Nantmawr, and a north-facing connection to the ONR at Llanymynech were all rejected.

Two WSMR bills were deposited on 10 November 1863 and the line to Llangynog was approved in the WSMR 1864 act, as were branches to a wharf on the Shropshire Union Canal and to the lime kilns at Nantmawr and Porthywaen. A connection with the ONR's Llanfyllin branch was also authorised. The WSMR was permitted to make use of the ONR's Llanymynech station and so much of the ONR's railway that would enable it to work trains from its existing railway to the branches. The ONR was excluded from using the Llangynog and Porthywaen lines but could use the remainder of the WSMR. The new works were to be capitalised at up to £200,000, with a further £66,000 permitted to be borrowed on mortgage.

The second 1863 bill became the Shrewsbury & North Wales Railway Act on the same day as the WSMR 1864 act. In addition to changing the SWMR's name, two more branches were authorised, both targeting sources of stone: the Breidden branch, from Kinnerley to 'a certain enclosure numbered 147 on the tithe commutation map', otherwise the hamlet known as Criggion, about 4½ miles, and the Nesscliffe branch, about 2½ miles. The SNWR was permitted some minor deviations and easing of curves and gradients of the 1862 route, the descriptions couched in such a way as to suggest that the original route had been examined and found not to be as practical as it might have been. Further share capital of £100,000, and borrowing of £33,000, was sanctioned, some of which could be raised by the creation of debenture stock. The LNWR was to be permitted to make use of the railway and the ONR's powers to use it were extended to include the deviations.

A year later, the SNWR was armed with further powers with an act that provided a hint that things were not going too well as another £100,000 capital and £33,000 borrowing were approved. The issue of preference shares was approved and the company could issue half shares, that is £5 instead of £10.

For every two half shares created, one would be designated the 'preferred share', the other the 'deferred share'. Whenever there were insufficient profits to pay a 5% dividend on the total, priority would be given to the preference shares; any deficiency was not allowed to be carried forward. Subject to approval at a general meeting, holders of existing shares could apply to have them divided. Again, further deviations were permitted, with two years allowed for the exercise of compulsory purchase powers, and four years for construction.

Receiving Parliamentary attention at the same time as the SNWR's 1865 act, and an integral part of this story, was a bill for the Shrewsbury & Potteries Junction Railway, enacted on 5 July 1865. The SPJR was intended to connect Shrewsbury with Stoke-on-Trent via a junction at Market Drayton. Its promoters were Michael Daintry Hollins, William Matthews, Richard Thomas Rowley, William Walter Cargill, Arthur Pittar Lattey and Henry Pelham Burn. Cargill and Lattey were involved with the WSMR. Amongst its several rail connections at Shrewsbury, the SPJR was empowered to make an independent line from a junction with the GWR/LNWR joint line from Shrewsbury to Wellington to Red Hill and make junctions there with the SNWR and the SWR. It was also empowered to make a branch from this line into Shrewsbury, terminating 'by a junction with the Shrewsbury & Hereford Railway near the south end of the viaduct of that railway adjoining the Abbey pool'. Some modifications to this route were approved in another SPJR act in 1866, when proposed branches to Minsterley and Bishop's Castle were rejected; they were intended to start from a junction with the SNWR's Moat Hall Tramway.

In parallel with the SPJR's 1866 act another SNWR act authorised a short branch near Llanymynech and yet more

Shrewsbury & Potteries Junction Railway 1865 proposals at Shrewsbury. *HLRO*

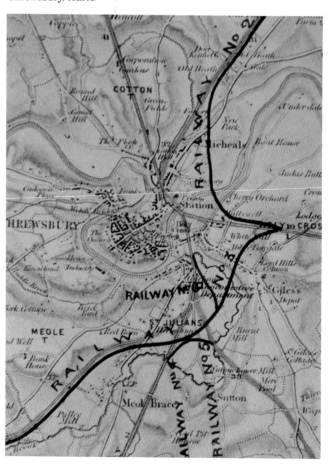

deviations, one of them to the Moat Hall Tramway which was required as a consequence of the SPJR connection at Meole Brace. Another £80,000 capital was authorised along with £26,000 borrowings. Several of the SNWR's proposals for this act were rejected, notably a line along the Meifod Valley that would have terminated in Llanfair Caereinion. The Shropshire Union Canal branch at Llanymynech, authorised in 1864, was abandoned.

A third act enacted on the same day, 16 July 1866, brought all the pieces together. The SNWR and the SPJR were amalgamated to create the Potteries, Shrewsbury & North Wales Railway, the original companies being dissolved. According to the act's preamble 'the railways of the North Wales company

Below: **Shrewsbury & Potteries Junction Railway 1866 proposals at Shrewsbury.** *HLRO*

Bottom left: **Shrewsbury & Potteries Junction Railway 1866 deviation proposals at Shrewsbury.** *HLRO*

Bottom right: **Shrewsbury & North Wales Railway 1866 proposals around Llanymynech.** *HLRO*

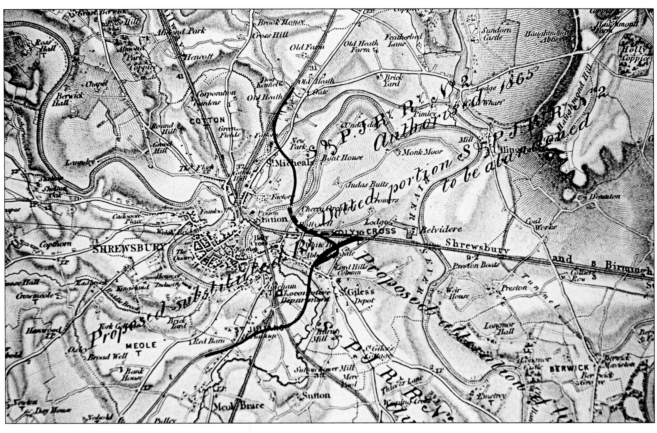

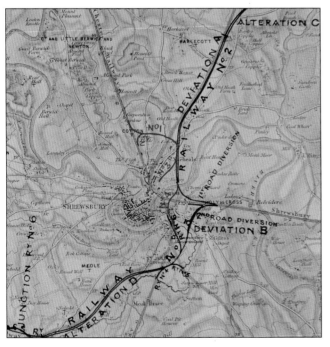

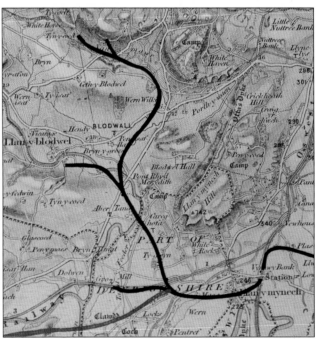

and the Potteries company could be worked with greater economy and convenience to the shareholders and the public if the same were placed under one management'. The directors of the dissolved companies became the new company's first directors until the first ordinary meeting after the passing of the act. The phoenix in the PSNWR's seal was obviously meant to symbolise the union but it was not born out of fire but of debt and that situation was never to be resolved.

The capital of the combined undertakings, plus that already sanctioned, was to be £950,000, including any capital authorised by the other 1866 acts, £80,000 from each. The combined capital previously authorised was summarised as comprising 10,000 £10

preference shares in the SNWR, 90,000 half shares of £5, 45,000 preferred and 45,000 deferred, representing the SNWR's ordinary capital, and 40,000 £10 shares in the SPJR. This act was very specific about the allocation of profits. Naturally the preference shares had priority for 5% but again no deficiency could be carried forward. Although the ordinary shares of the SNWR and PJSR were then ranked equally, SNWR £5 preferred shares had priority over the remainder.

Examining this Parliamentary activity, of nine acts to date, there does not appear to have been much in the way of strategic thinking, with amendments to routes being proposed within months of approval being given to them. The extensions and branches being thrown off in all directions must be a symptom of the difficulty being experienced in selling shares in the undertakings – add new destinations and people who might use the services might invest in them. It was stated in 1888 that shares and debentures had been sold at a discount although lists of stocks issued do not show any discrepancy with the capital available to the company. Another example of the lack of strategy is demonstrated by the existence of unused SNWR tickets.

The London Financial Association was responsible for supplying £200,000 of capital, repayable over 50 years, the length of France's Nantmawr leases. In 1865, Brown, Shipley & Co, described as 'general merchants in the city', loaned £100,000 to France against the security of £66,500 in debentures and £69,070

Left: **Potteries, Shrewsbury & North Wales Railway Company seal.** *National Archives*

Below: **Potteries, Shrewsbury & North Wales Railway as proposed.** *National Archives*

Right: **Shrewsbury & North Wales Railway Company seal.** *National Archives*

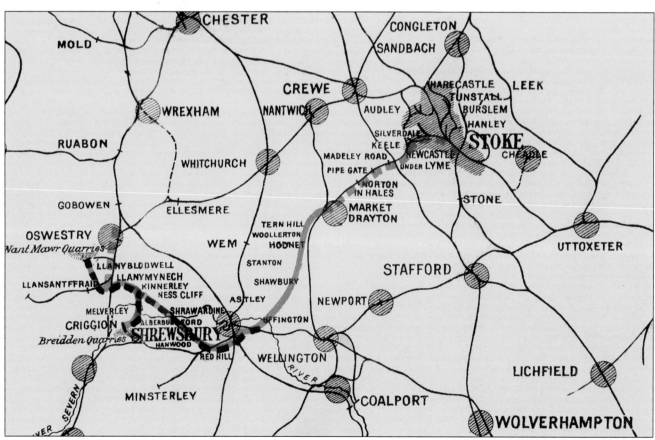

in shares in what became the PSNWR, £14,000 of Lloyds' bonds held by the Mold & Denbigh Junction Railway and £108,000 of MDR shares. It was intended that the lender should receive interest from France plus any dividend or interest payable on the various stocks.

The promotional costs must have been considerable, with every bill opposed by both the LNWR and the GWR allegedly working in collusion. When the junction was made at Red Hill the LNWR refused to permit its use and gave the Cambrian a rebate on traffic routed via the SWR to discourage it from making use of the PSNWR.

Construction had started around 1863. The directors' report to shareholders published in advance of the fourth ordinary meeting of the company held on 29 February 1864 stated: 'the contractor has used great energy in the construction of the line, which is now in a very advanced state. The whole of the land is in the possession of the contractor. Notwithstanding that some of the work has been of a more severe character than was anticipated, the directors have every confidence … that the line will be open during the ensuing summer.' In the same document the engineer, John Ashdown, reported that the earthworks between Red Hill and Shrawardine were well advanced despite one of the cuttings taking more effort than anticipated. The piers and cylinders of the Shrawardine river crossing were complete and most of the girders delivered and were in course of erection. The iron beams used in three bridges near Porthywaen, including that on France's Nantmawr quarry incline, were cast by William F. Sim & Co in Liverpool in 1865. At the time of the 1863 report the company had spent £129,537 15s 1d and had £1,862 4s 11d in hand.

Despite the board's confidence it was 1866 before the railway was ready to be opened. On 18 June 1866 SNWR company secretary Charles Chandler informed the Board of Trade (BoT) that the first part of the railway, from its junction with the SWR at Red Hill to its junction with the Cambrian at Llanymynech, would be ready for inspection on 26 June and requesting that it be conducted as soon as possible. On the same date John Wade, the SPJR's company secretary, wrote in similar terms regarding that line's works in Shrewsbury; Wade was an officer of the London Financial Association and became the PSNWR's secretary in 1872.

In sending the plans of both undertakings to the BoT on 21 June, incidentally, Ashdown, the engineer, noted that the 'Abbey yard branch' was to be used 'only temporarily as a passenger line pending the construction of other portions of the railways …'

Colonel F. H. Rich started the inspection on 3 July, taking two days and submitting his report on 8 July. Of the SNWR, he said that the line was 16m 24ch long, it was double track, with 70lb double-head rail laid in 28lb chairs spiked to transverse sleepers; it was 'well ballasted' with gravel. Turntables had been installed at Llanymynech and Shrewsbury. Of the nine overbridges four had brick arches, three had wooden decks on masonry abutments and two had cast-iron sides. There were 11 underbridges, two of brick, six with timber decks, and three with wrought-iron sides on masonry abutments: the greatest span was 32ft. He said that there were seven viaducts with a total of 24 openings, all quite small except that at Shrawardine which had two 60ft spans, two of 41ft 9in and two of 40ft 9in. It consisted of wrought-iron girders supported on cast-iron columns and masonry abutments. The other viaducts had both masonry columns and abutments. Some of these structures would have been flood relief channels in the vicinity of watercourses subject to flooding. He found that the works 'appeared to be substantially constructed and of sufficient strength'. An accommodation arch at 14m 9ch required pointing and watching.

There were no station buildings but platforms, signals and small timber booking offices had been provided. Ashdown undertook to complete some small works immediately: stops to all level crossing gates, to prevent them from being opened outwards; lamps to be placed on the gates; a handrail on the parapet of the underbridge at Hanwood to prevent passengers stepping out on to the parapet; the chains of the signal lamps to be marked so that the porter in charge could tell when they were home and the Breidden branch was to be guarded by a pair of facing points which were to be loaded and set for the main line. Clocks were to be supplied for the stations and the junction.

A pair of gates to close across the railway and road was to be erected at 'the public level crossing at 1m 50ch in the parish of Kinnerley and the lodge which is now building to be completed without delay'. He went on to say: 'These works can be done in a few days and the line may be opened for passenger traffic if their lordships are satisfied as to the public level crossings …' He had found seven crossings over public roads, one of which, near Ford, had not been specified in the legislation. He thought that the plans showed a bridge at the location, saying that the company should either prove that it was a private crossing or be required to provide gates and a lodge and then to undertake to submit a bill to Parliament 'next session' for approval. If approval was denied then the company should build a bridge within three months. Cae Gwynsyn crossing, between Maesbrook and Kinnerley, had only a small hut for the keeper, and he thought that the company should be required to undertake to build a lodge within three months.

Despite his earlier remark about the railway being fit for passenger traffic, Rich concluded that it 'cannot be opened for passenger traffic without danger to the public using the same by reason of the … the proper gatekeepers' lodge … and by reason of the unauthorised public level crossing …'

On 12 July 1866 Chandler was able to send the BoT a sealed undertaking, signed by the chairman, Elias Mocatta, and himself, to construct the lodge at Cae Gwynsyn within three months. He was also able to submit a certificate from the warden of Ford parish declaring that the road with the unauthorised crossing was used only as a public bridle road. The BoT replied by return that the line could be opened as soon as the works required by Rich had been carried out.

Of the SPJR between Red Hill and the Shrewsbury–Wellington line, sometimes known as the loop line, which was inspected at the same time as the SNWR, Rich said that it was 3m 25ch long with a 35ch branch to the Shrewsbury Abbey yard station. The gradient on the branch was 1 in 47, all trains were to be brought to a stand at the junction with the SPJR 'main line', and trains worked at very low speed into the station. There were two overbridges with stone abutments and cast-iron sides and five underbridges with stone abutments and wrought-iron girders. The largest span was 48ft. Once again the works appeared to be substantially constructed and of sufficient strength. Ashdown had undertaken to install spring buffers on the arrival platform and to take out a set of facing points by the junction at the top of the incline. With only these requirements, Rich was able to recommend that the SPJR could be opened to passenger traffic without danger to the public. Formal approval was given to the company on 14 July although it was 6 August before John Bucknall Cooper, the general manager, gave notice of the intention to open for passenger traffic on 13 August.

Making the railway double track between Llanymynech and Potteries Junction, on the Wellington to Shrewsbury line, was in anticipation of trains running through to Market Drayton and beyond and explains the easing of curves and gradients between Llanymynech and Red Hill. A yard with five sidings was established for the exchange of traffic at Potteries Junction, and wagon repairs were also carried out there. Coleham Junction was the name given to the divergence between the Abbey branch and the loop line.

The Criggion and Nantmawr branches, which took the railway into Montgomeryshire, although the latter quickly returned to Shropshire, had probably been opened for goods during 1865, with a service operated by France. The Criggion line was often referred to as the Breidden branch, Breidden Hill being the location of the quarry, Criggion the nearest community.

In addition to the terminals there were stations at Red Hill, Hanwood Road, Ford, Shrawardine, Nesscliffe (often misspelled Nesscliff by the railway), Kinnerley and Maesbrook. Whether the stations that were later established on the branches for passengers existed previously for goods traffic has not been established. As was so often the case in rural areas, none of the stations was particularly close to the places they purported to serve. Minimal facilities were provided for passengers although the houses constructed for the crossing keepers were quite substantial. There were considerable crossings of the Severn, at Shrawardine on the main line, and at Melverley on the Criggion branch. The Nantmawr quarry incline was not, incidentally, a part of the statutory railway although both France and the company considered it to be so; with no direct connection to the railway it was some 1,640ft long on a gradient of 1 in 7. The railway's total mileage was 28, of which 18 were used by passenger trains.

The first public timetable had five trains in each direction on weekdays and Saturdays and two return workings on Sundays. The 6am from Shrewsbury and return was the all-stations Parliamentary, 1d per mile for the labouring classes; on Sunday it left Shrewsbury at 8.30am. After an interval of four hours, the last return working left Shrewsbury at 7.30pm. The Sunday afternoon working to Llanymynech, surely an excursion, as it was over three hours before it returned, took 60 minutes, while the fastest working stopped only at Kinnerley and took 35 minutes. On the five-train service two train sets were needed so even with an unadvertised goods train service the PSNWR was not making good use of its double track.

Additionally, excursions to Criggion and Llanymynech were promoted on Thursdays in the railway's early years. According to Perkins, writing in 1903 (see Bibliography), through carriages worked between Oswestry and Shrewsbury but he did not state which company's vehicles did the through running. He also reported that from 26 August 1866 excursions were operated from Shrewsbury to Aberystwyth. In addition to the Parliamentary fares there were rates for three classes of passengers until second class was abolished during 1876.

With the railway open for traffic there were a number of problems with the PSNWR, some of which would pursue it for the rest of its existence. At £60,000 per mile to construct, it was claimed to be the most expensive railway in a non-metropolitan area in England. To service the capital and the debt at 5% would require some £60,000 profit per annum, a very unlikely outcome for an agricultural line.

Whether France was profligate in the PSNWR's construction can only be judged by analysing the construction costs, where known, or capital of other similar railways built at the same time. It was certainly not alone in being built with a double track formation. Possibly railway funds were used to build the Nantmawr quarry incline. The passage of time shows that France's stone and brick overbridges were quite sound, and most of them survive. Three of his iron beam bridges survive on the Nantmawr branch, one carrying modern traffic apparently unmodified, one requiring support to do so, while the third is an underbridge that now carries only light pedestrian traffic. Of his river bridges, that at Shrawardine lasted nearly 100 years before being rebuilt, only to be demolished shortly afterwards, and that on the Criggion branch obviously suffered by being built on the cheap, lasting only until c1910, when it was renewed, again cheaply.

The locomotives and rolling stock that France had used during construction became the company's operating stock but had been poorly maintained and were run down. The company had no working capital and quickly attracted £40,000 of court judgments against it. The landowners upon whose property the railway had been built remained unpaid. The most likely fruitful source of traffic, the Nantmawr quarry, was not obliged to use the line in its entirety and could bypass it at the whim of the quarry's proprietor, as proved to be the case.

After Overend, Gurney collapsed in May 1866 it was not long before France's own financial problems were manifest on the railway. He was engaged on constructing the Mold & Denbigh Junction Railway as well as the PSNWR east of Shrewsbury and work was stopped during the year. A notice that three inspectors of France's affairs in bankruptcy had been appointed was published in the *London Gazette* on 14 August 1866. According to a report in the *Railway Times,* a debenture holder obtained judgment in a claim against the company and issued a writ.

After bailiffs tried to seize a train that was in service agreement was reached for it to continue under the supervision of one of them, who was allocated a first class compartment. Later in the day the train called at Kinnerley where shunting was carried out. When the bailiff eventually looked out of the window to ascertain the reason for the delay he saw that the train was departing, leaving his carriage behind! He found the station locked up and unmanned and had to walk the 12 miles back to Shrewsbury in the dark, a hazardous experience for the unprepared in the days before light pollution was heard of. On subsequent days he avoided the last carriage. A receiver, William Quilter, was appointed on 11 December and the railway was closed on 21 December 1866.

The returns show that maintenance remained France's responsibility until 1869. During 1867 'locomotives engaged in construction work' hauled 4,067 tons, 2,000 tons less than during the brief operating period of 1866 when a loss of £99 had been incurred on income of £1,076; not a good omen for the future. There was no recorded traffic at all during 1868.

THE MAIN LINE – SHREWSBURY TO KINNERLEY

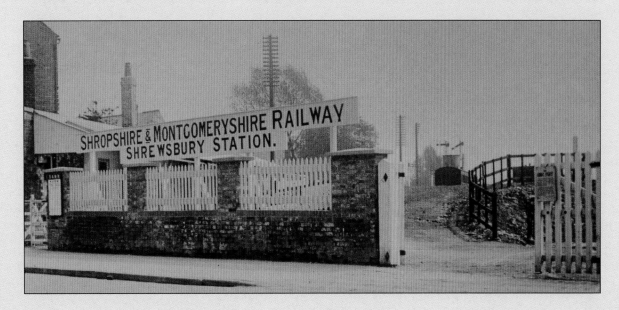

Top: **Shrewsbury station from the road with the station building's canopy visible on the left.** *WEH-LYN collection*

Above: **Shrewsbury, looking towards the stopblocks. There is evidence on the ground of locomotive fires having been cleaned and a Sentinel steam lorry, made in Shrewsbury, can be seen in the yard to the right.** *A. M. Davies collection*

Left: **Shrewsbury station buildings.** *Historical Model Railway Society*

Above: **On 20 March 1960, just before the line was closed, there was still stock in Shrewsbury station. During the period of military operation a second water tank had been installed and the track to the right of the water tower was removed. The platform road was relaid in flat-bottom rail while the loop and sidings still used older material.**
Brian Hilton/Author's collection

Right: **The SMLR's connection to the outside world, at Meole Brace.** *WEH-LYN collection*

Below right: **A halt at Meole Brace was added by the SMLR, conveniently located under the road bridge.**
A. M. Davies collection

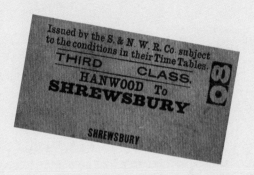

Top: **Red Hill was renamed Hookagate in 1920. One of the 'Continental style' signals provided at request stops is shown to advantage *c*1911. No instructions regarding their use have been found.** *A. M. Davies collection*

Left: **Edgebold, formerly Hanwood Road, after closure.** *A. M. Davies collection*

Below: **Ford & Cross Gates station, showing the passing loop and the platform at two levels.** *WEH-LYN collection*

Above: **Shrawardine Viaduct.**
A. M. Davies collection

Right: **The 1915 accident on Shrawardine Viaduct, showing 0-6-2T No 6 *Thisbe* and some of the stock badly askew.** *A. M. Davies collection*

Below: **This photograph, taken in difficult circumstances, shows that re-railing the train would have been no easy matter (see p.72).** *A. M. Davies collection*

Below right: **Shrawardine looking towards Shrewsbury, showing military trackwork and water tank in the 1950s. The station house remains in occupation.** *A. M. Davies*

Top: **Shrawardine platform, 1911. T. R. Perkins stands by the signal, with the station agent in the doorway.** G. *M. Perkins*

Above: **Nesscliffe & Pentre station on a summer's day between the wars, here using the spelling Nesscliff.** *T. R. Perkins*

Left: **During the 1950s, Nesscliffe & Pentre was the domain of station agent E. N. Fardoe.** *A. M. Davies*

Above: **Looking eastwards from the Kinnerley road bridge, September 1935.** *WEH-LYN collection*

Right: **Kinnerley station retained its LNWR poster board as well as its LMS replacement as late as 1937.** *G. Harrop/E. M. Johnson collection*

Below right: **One of the ex-LNWR 0-6-0s seen shunting at Kinnerley on 7 June 1938.** *Author's collection*

Top: **Scenes from the Kinnerley road bridge – 1. The Criggion branch diverged to the left at the western end of the station and also gave access to the SMLR's locomotive depot. Carriages were usually stabled in the Criggion bay platform.** *WEH-LYN collection*

Above: **Scenes from the Kinnerley road bridge – 2. Empty stone wagons.** *WEH-LYN collection*

Left: **This home-made ground frame shelter would have provided only partial protection from the elements.** *WEH-LYN collection*

Right: **Scenes from the Kinnerley road bridge – 3. A goods train in the station with a train approaching from Llanymynech.** *A. M. Davies collection*

Below: **Scenes from the Kinnerley road bridge – 4. Empty stone wagons and one of the ex-LNWR 0-6-0s. The sidings to the right contain empty stone wagons and loaded coal wagons.** *WEH-LYN collection*

Bottom: **An ex-LSWR 0-6-0 bound for Llanymynech. The number of observers standing on the bridge encourages the speculation that something unusual was happening. There are two men working on the crib erected under the water tower.** *WEH-LYN collection*

Left: **During the military occupation, Kinnerley's distinctive ground frame was removed from the platform and replaced by a cabin located opposite the Criggion branch junction.**
The view west on 21 September 1958. *R. F. Roberts*

Middle: **A quiet day at Kinnerley. Beyond the bridge a train is heading for Shrewsbury while one of the ex-LSWR 0-6-0s stands in the platform with a short goods train. A low-walled compound containing aggregate or sand has been erected at the end of the bay platform. Other photographs show what could be an end-loading ramp in this location.** *A. M. Davies collection*

Below: **Military signals and a block post can be seen in this 18 March 1960 photograph. There is only one arm on the gantry. The lamp that was on the platform has been removed. Hunslet 'Austerity' 0-6-0ST No 193 waits in the platform, probably with a special train.** *Hugh Ballantyne*

2

The Potteries, Shrewsbury & North Wales Railway

Despite the PSNWR being closed, attention was still being given to the uncompleted works at its eastern end, a bill being deposited, in December 1867, to sanction some minor changes to the authorised layout. Ashdown signed an estimate for a double-track 'substituted railway' 4f 6.30ch long, partly in cutting and partly on embankment that would have required four bridges. This replaced railway No 4 that had been authorised by the SPJR (Deviations) Act in 1866 and part of railway No 3 that had been authorised by the SPJR Act in 1865, and for the 'alteration of levels' on a single line over 3f 11ch distance, where the railway was to pass under Abbey Foregate, which would have required an earth cutting either creating or deepening and a footbridge. There were no objections to the bill so the act gained royal assent on 25 June 1868. In addition to approving the changes required, the act defined the route by which the PSNWR should cross the 'Shrewsbury and Birmingham railway of the London & North Western and Great Western Railways Companies' using a single span girder bridge of not less than 45ft width 'measured on the square' with a clear headway of not less than 15ft. Despite the lack of objection to the bill the PSNWR did not obtain the permission sought to extend the line in the time available to exercise compulsory purchase powers granted in the WSMR (New Lines) Act in 1864 in respect of two properties in Llanyblodwell.

It was not until 1868 that the PSNWR reached a settlement

Below: **Ex-LNWR No 1859 and train of four-wheeled carriages at Shrewsbury Abbey station in the early 1870s.** *Author's collection*

with its creditors. The scheme of arrangement that was devised was published on 28 January, confirmed on 9 May and enrolled on 13 July in accordance with the requirements of the Railway Companies Act of 1867. It made provisions for 'raising a sum of money not exceeding £70,000 by debenture stock, for the completion of certain portions of the company's undertaking and the payment of certain liabilities of the company, for converting the mortgage debt … into debenture stock, and for the issue of £60,000 in ordinary shares and of £19,800 in debenture stock, in satisfaction of certain other liabilities of the company, for the issue of a further sum in debenture stock in satisfaction of other liabilities of the company and for raising £200,000 … for the construction and completion of other portions of the company's undertaking'. The existing debentures, totalling £314,990, were classified 'B'; the £70,000 of new debentures were classified 'A', and the £200,000 of new debentures were classified 'C', £135,000 of which were issued. £151,800 ordinary shares authorised by the SPJR 1865 act which remained unissued were cancelled.

The Mid Wales Railway and Mold & Denbigh Junction Railway were also the subject of schemes of arrangement dealt with by the same solicitors on the same dates, and France was involved with both. It was December 1868 before PSNWR passenger services were resumed; the connection to the Wellington line was opened, but not that at Red Hill. The bridge over the Wellington line was not built.

It was no doubt the need to contain costs that led to the review

Left: **Employees pose for the photographer, *c*1879. The station offices were to the right; the Abbey's refectory pulpit is visible on the left.** *Author's collection*

Below: **The layout of the Abbey station in PSNWR times.**

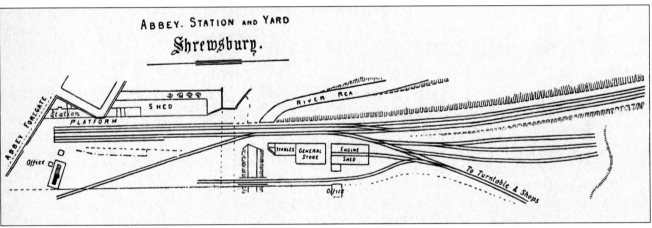

of the necessity for a double-track main line. On 18 September 1868, Chandler, writing from London, informed the BoT that the PSNWR intended 'to work a portion of the railway as a single line only' and asked if it needed to be re-inspected as a consequence. It took until 25 September before the BoT established its position, informing Chandler that 'the responsibility of working the railway as a single line must rest with the company and that the BoT cannot re-inspect it as their doing so might be held to imply that they approved the conversion of the double line into a single line'.

One would have thought that at the very least the BoT would have been interested in the operating procedures to be adopted following the singling. In the event, the line was singled between Ford and Llanymynech without the further involvement of the BoT.

After this retrenchment the expansion of services was on the agenda in 1869, for on 18 December Chandler wrote to inform the BoT that it was the intention of the directors to open a further portion of the railway, railways Nos 1 and 3 sanctioned by the WSMR (New Lines) Act in 1864, from Llanymynech to Llanyblodwell. He gave notice on 14 March 1870 that the branch would be ready for inspection from 20 March. By this time John Horn Tolmé had taken over as engineer and he submitted the plans, also on 14 March. Tolmé was a member of the Institution of Civil Engineers who later, in the 1870s, worked on the Hudiksvall–Herjeadalen Railway extension in Sweden.

Rich submitted his report on 29 March 1870. He reported that the lines were single with sidings at each end with land taken for a double track. The two railways were contiguous, from the point where railway No 1 made a junction with the Cambrian about 1,000yd west of Llanymynech station to where railway No 3 ended, for passenger purposes, at Llanyblodwell station.

Railway No 3 continued beyond Llanyblodwell for mineral trains only. Railway No 1 was 1m 7ch long and railway No 3 43ch long, the only station being Llanyblodwell.

The track consisted of 70lb double-head rail in 24ft lengths, fishplated and laid in 30lb chairs. The chairs were fixed to transverse sleepers with wrought-iron spikes, the half-round sleepers being laid at 3ft intervals. The steepest gradient was 1 in 88 and the sharpest curve, at the Cambrian junction, had a radius of 10ch. The line was well ballasted.

Six overbridges were constructed of brick and stone and a seventh had cast-iron girders. The single underbridge had stone piers and a timber deck. There were two timber viaducts that made crossings of the Afon Tanat. The viaduct on railway No 1 had seven 15ft spans and that on railway No 3 had five spans of 20ft. Rich found that the viaduct on railway No 3 was weak in the bearing beams and that there was lateral strain on the piles.

The aqueduct that carried the Montgomeryshire Canal over the railway at Wern consisted of an iron trough carried on wrought-iron girders. Its abutments were stone while the centre supports were iron columns. At Llanymynech, the branch made a double junction with the Cambrian, the points and signals being 'arranged on the locking principle'.

Llanyblodwell station, which consisted of a platform and signals was, like the rest of the branch, on a gradient of 1 in 88. The line was double in the station with catch points at the down end leading to a siding. Another trap point beyond the station prevented mineral wagons running through it. The formation beyond the station, to the Nantmawr quarries, was sufficient for just a single track although Rich did not comment on this feature.

Rich required the largest viaduct to be strengthened and

Right: **Abbey station shortly after abandonment. The coal merchant used the offices, stabling his horse in the booking office.**
T. R. Perkins collection

Below: **By June 1903 the canopy was in a very poor condition.**
G. M. Perkins

Llanyblodwell station to be provided with a booking hut and urinal. The track required 'a little packing and regulating'. He also required undertakings from the company regarding its method of operating the branch and that passenger trains would be worked only by tank engines. He was not yet prepared to sanction its opening for passenger trains.

Tolmé wrote that the viaduct had been strengthened and was ready for inspection on 7 April 1870. The undertaking that the railway would be worked with tank engines on the 'train staff system' was sealed on 16 April 1870. Following a further inspection Rich reported, on 20 April, that he had found the works in a satisfactory state and recommended that the line be opened for passenger traffic. The company was notified of this on 23 April 1870.

Events were nowhere near as straightforward when it came to having the Criggion branch approved for passenger traffic. On 28 May 1870, Chandler again wrote to inform the BoT that it was the intention of the directors to open a further portion of the railway, 'the Breidden branch, described as railway No 1 in the West Shropshire Mineral Railway (Branches etc.) Act 1864'. A second notice was submitted on 21 October, stating that the line would be ready for inspection from 24 October. Tolmé submitted

the plans, also on 21 October. Rich was instructed to make an inspection and submitted his report from Chester on 29 October.

The branch was, reported Rich, 5m 11ch long and single throughout with sidings. The track was the same as that used elsewhere on the PSNWR and broken stone had been used for ballast. The report stated the track required lifting and regulating and the ballast should be broken to a smaller size.

There were two bridges, one with stone abutments and seven brick arches, the other also with stone abutments but with a timber deck. There were two underbridges, one of timber, the other again with stone abutments and a timber deck. Rich described three timber viaducts, the largest with seven 38ft spans; the others had two and three spans respectively. 'These works appear to be of sufficient strength,' he said.

There were four level crossings over public roads, one of which had not been authorised. Local landowners had petitioned for a bridge but Rich thought that as the road crossing 'appears to be of small importance' it should be retained. The keeper lived nearby and the company would build a lodge if it was approved. One of Rich's colleagues would have none of it: a note appended to Rich's draft report declares 'The company should go to Parliament for authority to cross on the level'.

Another crossing that had been authorised did not, in Rich's opinion, cross a public road. The road served only a field and the gates had been locked against it for four or five years without any objection being made. The other crossings were satisfactory, with Rich noting that they were provided with 'good houses for the gate keepers'.

The stations were located at Melverley, Crew Green, Llandrinio Road and Criggion. 'They are incomplete and require clocks, well constructed platforms, shelter and booking offices ...' The junction at Kinnerley required signals to control the sidings in the vicinity of the junction and they were to be interlocked with the junction signals and the branch needed to serve a platform independently of the main line. The company had told Rich that it proposed to work the branch with one tank engine in steam. He was concerned about the branch's susceptibility to flooding, and advised the company to plan for such eventuality to prevent accidents.

He concluded by stating that due to the incompleteness of

the work the branch could not be opened for passengers without danger. The BoT would not endorse Rich's recommendation to accept the unauthorised crossing and required the company to seek Parliamentary approval within 12 months. The opening was therefore postponed for one month.

The company apparently did not attach any urgency to the BoT's requirements, for when Rich made his inspection on 29 November 1870 he found that none of the works reported as being incomplete had been executed. On receiving the second notification that the branch could not be opened to passengers Chandler wrote, on 8 December 1870, withdrawing the application.

It was 15 May 1871 before Chandler resubmitted the application, only to be met with a further rejection. Rich visited again on 22 May when he found that the platform at Kinnerley was too short; the signalling works had not been undertaken; a check rail was required for the loading dock siding, which was of 45ft radius; a handrail was required on an underbridge to prevent passengers from leaving a train there when the platform was extended; the other platforms were still deficient and the track and ballast had not received attention. Crew Green station required a gate on its access path and a handrail on the underbridge and a tree that obscured the view of the Llandrinio Road distant signal needed to be cut down. Rich restated the requirement for the company to make an undertaking concerning the unauthorised level crossing and also required a formal undertaking concerning the proposed method of working.

The PSNWR was obviously not deterred by this third rejection, for on 7 June 1871 Chandler requested further copies of the printed form that needed to be submitted to request an inspection. On 17 June Rich wrote from Dulwich that the works had been completed. He was able to recommend that the branch be opened for passenger traffic provided the company gave undertakings concerning the crossing, to work passenger trains with a tank engine, not to use the junction at Kinnerley for passenger traffic, and to work the branch on the train staff principle with only one engine in steam, or two engines coupled together. These requirements were communicated to the company on 22 June. The undertaking was sealed on 11 July and on 18 July 1871 the BoT gave its approval for the branch to be opened to passenger traffic.

France maintained his connection with the PSNWR despite his financial difficulties, entering into an agreement with it concerning the use of the Nantmawr branch and the quarry incline on 22 January 1872. He was to work the incline so long as he leased 'certain quarries called Nantmawr rocks'. The railway was to supply a weighbridge and additional rails to enable the incline to be widened.

The status of the second track became an issue again in July 1872. E. Elias, the general manager, had called to see Rich, seeking advice on how to proceed. The next day, on 24 July, he wrote to acknowledge a letter from Rich and to explain that the PSNWR board wished to single the line between Shrewsbury and Ford. It wanted to know whether it should first submit plans for approval or have the work done and then request the BoT to inspect it. Rich's letter is not on file but it seems likely that he had either not been available to see Elias or had refused to see him without an appointment. Elias concluded '... and pardon the trouble I have given you'.

Rich actually had no answer for Elias. The concept of a company with a double track wishing to reduce to a single line was clearly unknown. He sought advice from the BoT's secretary suggesting that if it was allowable then the PSNWR should be requested to submit plans. The advice received was that as a company could 'shut up a line entirely they can therefore, I imagine, convert a double line to a single one'. Rich's proposal concerning the submission of plans was supported.

Chandler gave notice of intention to proceed on 6 August 1872. Saying that it was intended to work the proposed single line with the 'train staff system', he explained that changes were intended to be made at Shrewsbury, Red Hill, Hanwood Road and Ford. It was not until 30 September 1873 that he was in a position to submit the formal second notice to request an inspection. Rich was unavailable so Colonel W. Yolland was deputed to make it. He submitted his report from Shrewsbury on 8 October 1873.

Noting that the line beyond Ford 'has long since been converted into, and worked as a single line' he explained that as

Above right: **A part of the Shrewsbury loop line, photographed in June 1903.**
G. M. Perkins

Right: **The Rea bridges at Shrewsbury. The PSNWR structure is in the foreground, the Shropshire Railways replacement, with a part of its parapet collapsed, behind.**
T. R. Perkins collection

there were only three passenger trains and two goods trains in each direction each day, 'there is no doubt that all the traffic can be safely worked on a single line'. However, he added: 'But the working of the traffic on a single, instead of on a double line is attended with increased risk to the public', requiring the company to undertake to work the traffic on the absolute block system combined with the train staff and ticket system.

On the ground, Yolland required a down home signal to be placed on the line from Wellington in advance of the fouling points at Abbey junction and opposite the home signal for the Abbey branch, the said home signal to be fully interlocked with others in the locality. One of the facing point switches was 'in a bad state' and needed to be replaced.

At Red Hill and Hanwood Road he required sidings, which connected to the single line, to be interlocked with the up and down signals so that nothing might leave the single line or the sidings except when the signals were at danger. He noted that the PSNWR did not intend to keep men stationed at these places.

A loop line at Ford intended for passing trains was about 100yd long; facing points at each end of the loop were required to be interlocked by the respective distant signals, and the signals with each other. Declaring that the works were incomplete, Yolland declined to approve the working of the line between Shrewsbury and Ford as a single line.

This left the PSNWR in a quandary. It had converted its line and it continued to work its traffic, yet the BoT would not sanction its use by passenger trains. John Wade, on Chandler's behalf, wrote on 14 October 1873 to say that he was instructed to state

that the company was prepared to give an undertaking to comply with Yolland's requirements 'as expeditiously as possible'. In the meantime, he asked 'whether the company is to discontinue to carry passengers until these works are completed or whether the BoT will be satisfied with the undertaking above mentioned'.

The BoT was prepared to be flexible and the next day informed Wade that it was prepared to sanction the working of the single line on receipt of a sealed undertaking and provided that both Yolland's requirements were carried out expeditiously and that he be permitted to make another inspection. In the meantime the company was to take every precaution to prevent accidents.

The PSNWR's London solicitors submitted the undertaking on 31 October 1873 and, beyond acknowledging its receipt the BoT, judging by the lack of correspondence in its files, and the PSNWR both appeared to forget about the matter. It does seem rather strange that the BoT apparently overlooked the previous correspondence concerning the double track and that Yolland was unaware that it had not been inspected. Similarly, the PSNWR's manager must have been unaware of the previous approach on the subject.

With or without approval, the PSNWR's main line was operated as a single-track line henceforth. There were passing loops at Ford, Shrawardine, Kinnerley and Llanymynech with run-round loops at the termini. The second platform at stations without loops was soon demolished.

The London Financial Association, which had put up money for the PSNWR's construction and held debentures as surety, had the PSNWR put into receivership on 30 January 1873, presumably because the debenture interest was unpaid. Wade was appointed receiver, responsible for day-to-day control of revenue and expenditure and the line was operated under the direction of the court. It does seem remarkable that the directors did not comment on this loss of control in their reports. Wade said, incidentally, in his affidavit to Parliament in 1881, that he did not publish reports during the receivership – that for the second half of 1878, certified as the last one produced by the company, has his printed signature on it.

It also seems bizarre that a company in receivership would promote a bill for an extension, as the PSNWR was to do later in 1873. Wade's accounts are held in the National Archives and reference is made to certain entries elsewhere. Some entries can be mentioned here: payments totalling £66 13s 4d annually to the Mid Wales Railway Co, rental for an office; £20 paid for a (very expensive) cow killed on the railway, and, on

Above: **Meole Brace, looking westwards with the GWR/LNWR Shrewsbury–Welshpool joint line on the right, separated by the troublesome fence from the abandoned PSNWR. The latter looks as though it was being used as a thoroughfare. A junction between the two railways was made just beyond the footbridge in 1911.**
T. R. Perkins collection

Right: **The site of Red Hill station as seen in June 1903. The overturned ground frame was still there in 1911.**
T. R. Perkins collection

Richard Reeves, the former PSNWR guard on the inspection trolley near Hanwood Road station in June 1903. The bridge's brick arch was built by Chambers for the Shropshire Railways, replacing the original timber structure. *F. E. Fox-Davies*

11 November, £10 to Reverand J. Luxmore, a donation for the widow Jeffreys.

The PSNWR's relationship with France was not an easy one. It appears that his activities east of Shrewsbury, including a crossing of the Severn, had been started on his own initiative. When he sought further funding from the London financiers responsible for most of the PSNWR's capital they, possibly conscious of the railway's parlous financial position, refused, leading France to threaten to withdraw the Nantmawr stone traffic.

According to Cooper, in Parliament in 1888, France carried out his threat in 1872, routeing his stone via the Cambrian at Llanymynech, although Cooper said that when he did send his traffic over the railway he did so inconsistently: 1,000 tons one week, nothing the next. Cooper went on to become the manager of the Belfast Central Railway and then the Stafford & Uttoxeter Railway before joining the Neath & Brecon Railway. He was replaced by Elias, already encountered, who was replaced by Albert Judd, previously an employee of the Monmouthshire Railway, in 1874.

Looking at the traffic returns it is difficult to identify the effect of France's behaviour on the PSNWR's business at 'that' time. Revenue from mineral traffic rose each year until 1874 when it dropped back by some £2,500 only to peak at £6,966 in 1875. The peaks and troughs of tonnage carried match those of revenue when it might be expected that if France's traffic was being carried only to Llanymynech the tonnage would remain the same, or similar, but that the revenue would fall.

Only in 1875, when 126,312 tons of stone were carried, did the correlation between volume and revenue alter, which might be accounted for either by some of it being carried a shorter distance, but goods train mileage was increased by 10,000 during

the year, or a reduced rate being chargeable because of the increased volume. The latter seems more likely; the PSNWR would have been some £1,500 better off had the 1874 average rate been charged. The board attributed the 1874 reduction to the 'unsettled state of affairs in south Staffordshire'; during that year the railway carried 34,000 tons of stone less than it had done the year before, but its goods trains operated 2,000 miles more.

However, stone traffic in 1876 was less than half that of the year before and then fell to less than 20,000 tons in 1877, a poor year for all of the PSNWR's traffic. Whereas the other traffic recovered to near 'normal' levels in 1878/9 the stone traffic did not, achieving less than 25,000 tons in those years. So, if France's activities did affect the PSNWR it was from 1876, not from 1872. The last payment made to him for working the incline was in May 1876.

Meanwhile, in 1873, expansion in a new direction was being promoted, when a bill was deposited for a 3½-mile extension from the Nantmawr branch, 'near the mile post denoting 21¼ miles from Shrewsbury', to Treflach and Trefonen, at an estimated cost of £47,406. The latter is today a sizeable village with a population in the locality of nearly 4,000 recorded in the 2001 census. France leased a colliery between the two villages from Sir Watkin Wynn from c1870. The extension would have entailed a steep gradient and a reverse that not altogether coincidentally took it close to the Nantmawr quarry. This was an expensive way of avoiding the troublesome incline when there might have been an easier way to connect the colliery to the rail network. Apart from the need to establish that only five houses inhabited by eight 'persons of the labouring classes' were affected by the proposed route, there were no problems in gaining the act, which received royal assent on 21 May 1874.

The £50,000 capital required was to be kept separately as the 'Trefonen extension capital' and the operating receipts and expenses were also to be accounted for separately. An unusual article was the requirement for the extension to be worked efficiently and for the company to develop the traffic.

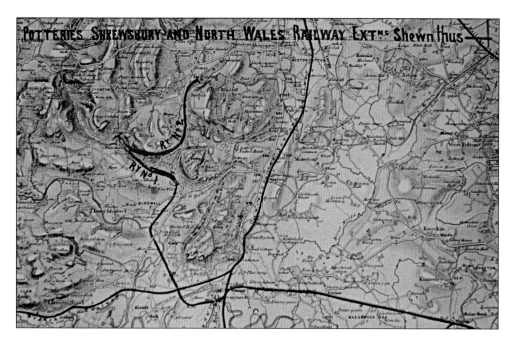

PSNWR proposed extension to Treflach and Trefonen, 1873.
HLRO

On application by an aggrieved party, including lenders and shareholders, the BoT could appoint an arbitrator to resolve any disputes. On 6 August 1873 the PSNWR had made an agreement with France concerning the connection of the Nantmawr quarries to the Trefonen extension by a tramway in order to avoid the incline. In his petition submitted in objection to the 1881 winding-up act France asserted that some works on the extension, including road diversions, had been made but at the hearings he denied that claim; Wade said that the PSNWR had taken no action to exercise its powers under the act but that France had obtained leases of quarries and land adjoining the proposed route and had then altered roads and laid rails without any authority from the company to do so.

That the PSNWR had limited resources to maintain its stock is suggested by a payment of £81 8s 3d to Beyer, Peacock & Co for 'repairing engines etc.' on 14 July 1873. Other payments two days earlier, to the Birmingham Tube Co for '150 iron tubes', £72 9s, and to T. Turton & Son for 'spring steel for locomotives and wagons', £16 6 9d, give an indication of the work that might have been carried out. In January 1875 the GWR was paid £2 2s 6d for 'repair of locomotive power'. In May 1875 payments totalling £73 10s were made to the GWR for 'engine hire', more likely to be for locomotives than stationary engines; these entries became a regular feature of the accounts. It may not be unconnected that the locomotive fleet had been reduced to four from seven up until 1872, or that payments for *Hope* had ceased after January 1875.

Although the PSNWR and the BoT had ceased to communicate on the issue of singling the main line the two organisations continued to be in contact, particularly in 1875/6, when three accidents were reported.

● A PSNWR mineral train was in a collision with three wagons that had run away from an LNWR goods train on 16 October 1875. The driver was killed and the fireman injured. The cause of the collision 'appeared to be the want of proper arrangements, such as catch points, at the south end of the Potteries goods yard and neglect of the proper precaution on the part of the second brakesman of the LNWR train for the safety of the wagons'. Rich, who inquired into the accident, concluded: 'The arrangements of the Potteries yard were not subjected to the inspection of a government officer as the yard in question forms a portion of a mineral line which is not used for passenger traffic.'

● On 29 December 1875 a passenger train from Llanymynech to Shrewsbury had been left standing opposite Coleham Junction signalbox when it was run into at low speed by a mineral train from Nantmawr which failed to stop; four passengers were injured. The collision was the result of the driver of the mineral train not having brought his train under proper control soon enough when approaching the junction. Yolland established that the worked-distant signal was not working because the signalman had not oiled its mechanism and had not bothered to light its lamp. The permanent way engineer told Yolland that it was not the custom to use the signal, and had it been functioning properly the locomotive driver might have been prompted to start braking earlier. He also found that the passenger train had been left at the junction while its locomotive took two loaded cattle vans to Potteries Junction. Yolland concluded his report: 'It is quite useless to recommend that this line should be worked on the block system in addition to the train staff and ticket system. I understand that it does not pay its working expenses and it is evident that the means now provided for working the traffic safely are not made use of.'

● On 10 July 1876 a man without a ticket got into the brake van of a special train at Shrewsbury unseen by the guard. He fell out of it between Shrewsbury and Red Hill, breaking his leg. The BoT found no need for further inquiry into the incident.

As the years passed, the PSNWR became completely isolated from its railway neighbours. There was a fence separating it from the parallel Shrewsbury & Welshpool line between Shrewsbury and Red Hill. The joint lines saw fit to complain to the BoT about it on 3 June 1876, when they said that it was defective and not stock-proof. Yolland was sent to inspect it although the BoT initially thought that it was beyond its legal remit. As the line had been opened as recently as 1866, Yolland reported, the fence should still be in good order if it was originally sound. He found that the repairs being carried out when he visited would still not be cattle-proof and notified Judd accordingly. The joint lines had followed up their complaint by notifying the BoT of the eight occasions since 1866, seven of them since 1870, that animals had got onto the Wellington line at Potteries Junction. The joint lines then offered to pay for a gated fence to be built, partially on PSNWR land, at Potteries Junction, Judd advising them that it would be protected by the existing distant signal at the bridge

over Sparrow Lane. At some unknown date the Nantmawr branch was also gated near Llanymynech.

It must have become apparent to the PSNWR board and its shareholders from a very early date that the railway was not a viable business. Even in the worst years the majority of its revenue came from stone yet it did not have the benefit of most mineral railways, a monopoly of the traffic. In the best years the railway was still unable to make a profit, never mind service its considerable debt; by 1875 debenture interest was £168,055 3s 8d in arrears. Of the five locomotives available to the company in 1875 one was hired and three were 'vested in trustees'. Wade recorded monthly payments totalling £14 13s 4d to Brown, Shipley & Co and £29 6s 8d to the London Financial Association for the hire of the locomotive *Hope,* payments which, as already noted, ceased after January 1875.

All 13 carriages and three passenger vans were hired, as were 100 wagons, five covered goods wagons and five cattle trucks, while ten timber trucks, one goods brake van, 40 lime wagons and a further 212 wagons were vested in trustees. The purchase lease for carriages, wagons and vans cost £544 6s 8d annually. Wade's accounts show that cattle wagons were hired from the Bishop's Castle Railway at an annual cost of £45. The Midland Wagon Co was paid £374 0s 3d for wagon hire in April 1873, £368 18s 9d on 12 June 1873 and £368 18s 9 on 12 March 1874. As the wagon fleet was not reduced after these payments ceased it may be that ownership was transferred during 1874. In 1879 £2 was paid to the LNWR for the hire of a coach.

According to the railway's returns to the BoT a locomotive was disposed of during each of the three years from 1873 and the carriage fleet was reduced by five vehicles in 1877. After the stone traffic collapsed in 1876 trains were run mixed, but the all-round reduction in expenses that followed still did not bring the railway to profit.

On 30 June 1876, the PSNWR withdrew from membership of the Railway Clearing House, leading to the loss of through rates for traffic booked for non-PSNWR destinations, as a consequence of the RCH increasing the level of members' surety from £500 to £1,500. France complained about the effect on his rates, probably making him less competitive, but Wade responded by pointing out that without membership the railway's losses were reduced.

Contrary to what might have been expected, it was not the PSNWR's impoverished finances that brought about its closure but a complaint from a member of the public concerned about the condition of the river bridge on the Criggion branch. On 24 April 1880 a doctor from Worcester, Hector Swete, informed the BoT that he had become concerned about the 'apparently rotten condition' of the bridge when he visited the locality to collect samples of river water in connection with Liverpool Corporation's Vyrnwy reservoir scheme. He had walked over the bridge and found that part of the flooring had fallen into the river. 'To my eye, uneducated in engineering, the whole structure appears frightfully rotten ...' The BoT sent a copy to Wade, who replied that he had written to Judd about it and undertook to submit it to the directors at their next meeting.

The directors met on 25 May; Judd submitted a report on the bridge and said that it was safe for traffic. He was ordered to report further on the bridge, whether any further repairs were necessary and to take such steps as he deemed advisable to ensure the safe conduct of traffic. Wade sent a copy of the minute to the BoT. Although, on the face of it, this was a satisfactory response the BoT obviously had doubts. On 27 May, Rich was ordered to inspect the railway at the earliest opportunity.

Rich submitted his report from Shrewsbury on 9 June 1880. The file copy is obviously his draft and was written in haste, lacking sufficient clarity to permit all of it to be quoted verbatim; italics represent Rich's own emphasis.

He had found that the bridge's timber was so badly decayed that part of it had given way and been 'supported in a temporary

Left: **Kinnerley station seen during the winter of 1902/3; hay has been stacked under the bridge.** *F. E. Fox-Davies*

Below: **Kinnerley signalbox with a fallen signal post to its left, winter 1902/3.** *F. E. Fox-Davies*

manner'. The longitudinal timbers that carried the rails were 'quite rotten'. The bridge was not level and about 1ft out of line. Despite branch traffic being worked with 'a small contractors' engine that weighs about 10 tons, *I do not consider this bridge safe for traffic'*. He went on to say that the wooden parts of all the PSNWR bridges required repair or renewal except some between Kinnerley and Llanymynech that had been renewed. The branch sleepers were decayed and required complete renewal. The fencing was incomplete and signals, level crossing gates and timber station platforms were in need of repair and 'in many cases they should be renewed. The rails are out of line ... *I do not consider this branch fit or safe to carry traffic.'*

As regards the main line, the masonry, brickwork and ironwork were all good, although the latter required cleaning and painting. Some settlement in the wing walls of the bridges needed pointing. '... *but the wooden decking, the wooden cross bearers and the longitudinals on the bridges require a thorough repair and in many cases the whole of the hard wood should be renewed.* The sleepers were generally covered with ballast,' he continued, 'but where they are exposed ... they are much decayed. Many require renewal.

'The best and cheapest plan,' he thought, 'would probably be to re-lay the railway. The fencing, the signals, the points and locking bolts and bars and the wooden platforms at the stations require repairing. *Some of the piles in the first underbridge next to the Abbey station, which consists of five openings of 15ft and some of the wooden piles in a high wooden bridge of some 15ft openings over the River Tanat require repairs and renewal.*

'Some of the level crossing gates require renewal and others require to be repaired. This railway,' Rich concluded, 'requires to be thoroughly overhauled and repaired. The rails should be lifted and regulated and the damaged rails should be taken out and renewed. The ... line was originally well made. The traffic is small and worked at low speed'.

The report was immediately sent to Wade but it was 18 June

before be replied with the directors' observations: 'I am desired by the directors ... to inform you that they have spent all the moneys received from traffic and other sources after payment of the working expenses and that there are no funds in the hands of the receiver available for carrying out the large and extensive repairs advised by Colonel Rich. Under these circumstances the directors desire to place themselves in your hands and would be glad to know whether you would recommend the whole of the line to be closed or only that portion known as the Breidden branch. I may add that the directors have kept the line open for some years past solely to accommodate the district and they will co-operate with the BoT in any way you can suggest by which the inconvenience caused by the cessation of the goods and passenger traffic may be lessened.

'May I request the favour of an early reply as the directors do not wish in any way to incur personal responsibility by allowing the trains to run over a line which is not perfectly safe.'

In fact, the Breidden branch was closed to passengers the same day, Judd having published a notice to that effect on 14 June(page34). The branch goods service, however, would continue to operate on Wednesdays and Saturdays 'as heretofore'.

The BoT's response was immediate. First, a telegram: 'By order of the board and at the request of the Board of Trade you are forthwith to suspend all traffic on the railway. Attend board at 10.30 tomorrow. Telegraph if you have received and carried out above order.' And secondly, a letter: 'I am directed by the Board of Trade to acknowledge receipt of your letter of the 18th inst stating the inability of the Potteries, Shrewsbury & North Wales Railway Company to carry out the works considered necessary by Colonel Rich for putting the railway into a safe condition for public traffic and asking the advice of the Board of Trade in the matter. In reply I am directed by the Board of Trade to inform you as stated in the telegraph forwarded to you this morning that the responsibility of allowing the line to fall into its present condition and the working of it whilst in this condition must remain with the directors but the Board of Trade have no hesitation in saying in reply to your letter that having regard to the public safety the line should be closed at once. The Board of Trade would be glad to learn with the least possible delay what steps have been taken.'

Both were sent on 19 June. Wade replied on 22 June: 'I am instructed by my directors to acknowledge receipt of your telegram and letter of the 19th inst stating that the BoT had no hesitation in saying that the line should be closed at once and to inform you that in consequence of such telegram and letter my directors gave immediate instructions for closing the line and that all traffic is now stopped.' Shortly afterwards, an agreement was made with the Cambrian whereby that company would work and maintain the Nantmawr branch for a period of two years, paying the PSNWR 3d per ton. Elsewhere, everything was left just as it had been on 19 June.

Two parties were sufficiently inconvenienced by the closure to write to the BoT with ideas to circumvent it: the Bradford Estate, at Knockin, and the Midland Railway Carriage & Wagon Co, at Shrewsbury. The former, on seeking permission to work a horse tram between Llanymynech and Kinnerley to transport domestic coal was told that it was a matter for the company. The latter sought to make use of the section of the PSNWR between its works adjacent to the Abbey station and the junction with the LNWR (sic) to transport its goods and materials; the BoT had no power, the company was informed.

The BoT's requirements seemed quite unequivocal: the railway must be closed. The PSNWR even went so far as to remove lengths of rail at strategic places to inhibit unauthorised movements. Yet when the BoT was approached by France, amongst others, it replied: 'The Board did not order, and had no power to order, the closing of the railway'. Indeed, on 26 June it had written to Wade '... your directors to be so good as to cause the BoT to be informed what steps they propose to take to put the line in question in a proper state of repair.'

Of course, the BoT had ordered the railway to be closed, but only for so long as it took for it to be returned to a state of good repair, being unaware of the share and debenture holders' loss of will to spend more money on their failed investment.

In November, the debenture holders agreed, at a meeting, to promote a bill to allow the railway to be sold and to sanction the company's winding up. At a hearing held before a House of Lords select committee over several days in July 1881, objections were presented from 'Humphrey Purnell Blackmore and others', and the 'Imperial Credit Company and another'. Blackmore had been the agent through whom the £100,000 had been loaned to France by Brown, Shipley & Co (BS) in 1865.

Francis Alexander Hamilton was the senior partner at BS. He explained the background to the loan and said that although France had paid interest on the loan before his bankruptcy, no dividends or interest had been paid on the securities. He and the other debenture holders were willing to forgo 75% of their investment, he said, if it meant that the railway could be sold.

In an attempt to make the Nantmawr incline part of the PSNWR undertaking France was examined on the nature of the 1872 and 1873 agreements. The proposal was struck out due to the failure to give notice and produce plans.

Lord Bradford explained, in the House of Commons, that some 30 acres of his land had been taken by the PSNWR and had not been paid for. He thought that the closure of the line was a 'very great injury' to the public.

France was called as an objector to the bill; in financial difficulties again, his objection was enjoined by his trustees.

Shrawardine Viaduct seen from the north in June 1903.
F. E. Fox-Davies

Following the BoT's instruction to close the railway the PSNWR had instructed him to cease using the incline. His objection was to preserve his rights under the agreement. He did not like the agreement and felt constrained by it but feared its loss, as without it he thought that he could be prevented from exporting his stone

via the incline. He thought that the PSNWR had not kept its side of the bargain by its alleged failure to carry out contracted works on the incline. He had done some of them himself but had not been reimbursed the £210 they had cost him.

France described his quarries and their relationship to the incline in some detail. He went on to say that although he had worked the incline he would prefer not to: 'It is an exceedingly risky business even with all the care we take and we have killed men to do it. We get runaways. We let down at a time 5 ton 10 [cwt] on each wagon. You see the character of these wagons. We cannot use railway wagons there at all.' He paid 3d per ton to use it and considered that the supply of horses and men to move wagons to and from the incline a function of working it.

The quarry's own wagons were used on the incline, the contents then being tipped into PSNWR wagons; he had tried to get the drops altered as the existing arrangement had a fall of up to 75ft and converted too much of his stone to chippings.

He was hoping that the Cambrian would take over the responsibility for the incline in addition to the Nantmawr branch; if it would not he would, for 1d per ton. He asserted that the branch and incline had never been inspected and that the BoT had no interest in mineral lines, only in passenger lines. The BoT telegram and letter to the PSNWR had been read out earlier, when the chairman ruled that the telegram was unequivocal that the railway was to suspend 'all traffic'.

The London Financial Association came under attack from France, who claimed that the association was using its influence with the PSNWR in an attempt to take over his quarries by increasing the rates and by discouraging the Cambrian and the GWR from taking over the Nantmawr branch.

The PSNWR's barrister tried to claim that France had no right to be heard on the subject of the agreement, arguing that as France had mortgaged two of the quarries he was no longer the lessee as defined by it. France got his protection.

The PSNWR winding-up act received the royal assent on 18 July 1881. The company could be wound up and the liquidator

---

Potteries, Shrewsbury and North Wales Railway.

NOTICE!

The Railway Company hereby give Notice that on and after Wednesday, June 16, they will cease to run Passenger Trains on their Railway between Kinnerley and Criggion, commonly called the Breidden Branch. The said Breidden Branch Railway will however be worked for Goods and Mineral Traffic on Wednesdays and Saturdays as heretofore.

A. JUDD,

GENERAL MANAGER.

Abbey Offices,
June 14th, 1880.

F. A. JONES, PRINTER, SHREWSBURY.

could sell the railway. Of particular interest is article 8, application of purchase money, because it severely restricted the options of both the liquidator and any prospective purchaser. Any monies received had to be dispensed in the following order of priority:

1 Costs of the act and the winding-up.
2 Compensation and expenses for completing the purchase of land taken by the PSNWR.
3 'A' class debenture stock, up to 60% of the holding providing three quarters of holders discharge, in writing, any claim for principal or interest.
4 'B' class debenture stock, up to 40% of the holding providing ...
5 'C' class debenture stock, up to 25% of the holding providing ...
6 The company's creditors, up to 20% of the debt, providing the majority in number and value relinquish any further claim
7 Share and stockholders, up to 7% of the holding, subject to majority agreement at a special meeting. If the purchase money was insufficient to pay the percentages then they would be reduced in proportion.
8 Any balance to be distributed to share and stockholders in proportion to their holdings, in addition to any sums due by application of the previous section.

This effectively set a minimum price of around £300,000 for the railway and limited the liquidator's scope for negotiation. No one was likely to agree to accept less than the specified percentage and the requirement to pay the landowners in full would always be a sticking point. He was also restricted by article 4, which ruled that the PSNWR could be sold only to another railway, removing the options of either selling part of it or selling it for scrap.

A remarkable feature of the winding-up act was its description of the PSNWR: 'And whereas for some years the said receiver has been enabled to keep up a small but inefficient service of trains only by devoting the whole of the said tolls and receipts of the company's undertaking to the mere running expenses, and by neglecting the maintenance and repair of the permanent way and bridges, but having no funds to execute certain repairs deemed necessary ... the railway was ... closed to public traffic ... and has since remained so.'

The PSNWR company was ordered to be wound up on 21 April and on 8 July 1882 Alexander Young, a partner in the chartered accountants Turquand, Young & Co, was appointed liquidator. He was to say that he was appointed because the judge knew him and not the other candidates. His firm became, via several amalgamations, a part of the international accountancy practice Ernst & Young. Wade's accounts were completed at the end of 1882. There was sufficient income from rentals to pay for the locomotives to be looked after in the PSNWR's locomotive shed at Shrewsbury and to keep the boundary fences under repair. The coaching stock was stored outside, at Shrewsbury, where the elements and vandalism gradually took their toll. The connection with the Shrewsbury–Wellington line was lifted, presumably by the LNWR/GWR, and the boundary fenced. At Llanymynech the Cambrian made unofficial use of some of the sidings for stock storage purposes. Elsewhere the railway became overgrown.

John Parson Smith became the lessee of the Nantmawr quarry *c*1885. The quarry and branch had been out of use for some time, and on 24 July he agreed to pay the Cambrian £800 to put the Nantmawr branch into good repair to carry the stone traffic.

The Cynicus series of postcards featured a number of bucolic railways, this one allegedly representing the PSNWR. This particular copy is of interest because it was sent by local enthusiast F.E. Fox-Davies on 17 May 1911, when the line was being reconstructed for the SMLR. In his message he wrote that he visited Kinnerley regularly and had been to the loco shed 'yesterday' to enquire about loco No 2 which had not then arrived. *Author's collection*

OUR LOCAL EXPRESS.
Potteries Railway—
Llanymynech to Shrewsbury

THE MAIN LINE – WERN LAS TO LLANYMYNECH

Above: **Wern Las platform in September 1938.**
WEH-LYN collection

Right: **Wern Las siding seen in September 1935.**
WEH-LYN collection

Below: **Maesbrook station and the crossing keeper's house, Easter 1911. The station agent, Mrs Watkins, poses with a flag for the photographer.**
F. E. Fox-Davies

Above: **Maesbrook before the War Office arrived and relaid the track.** *D. Cairns*

Left: **Maesbrook in 1958. A Drewry railcar may be discerned in the distance.** *A. M. Davies*

Below: **One of French's overbridges between Maesbrook and Llanymynech in September 1935; the brickwork on the parapet might be attributed to Chambers.** *WEH-LYN collection*

Left: **A view along the track between Maesbrook and Llanymynech, probably from the same bridge, also in September 1935.**
WEH-LYN collection

Below: **The approach to Llanymynech seen from the Cambrian/GWR station footbridge; the home signals can be seen amongst the trees to the right. A coal yard has been established on the site of the former PSNWR locomotive shed.**
John Keylock collection

Bottom: **By the mid-1950s the cabin had been demolished and the signals were gone.**
Historical Model Railway Society

Above: A 1911 view of Llanymynech station with the building freshly painted and the old locomotive shed still in place. *T. R. Perkins collection*

Left: A later view shows that although the 1911 station nameboard has been consumed by greenery, a new, and much larger board promotes the SMLR as the shortest route to Shrewsbury, with 'frequent trains, cheap fares'. As there were usually only four trains per day to Shrewsbury the use of the word 'frequent' seems imaginative. The track looks as though it might have been re-sleepered and ballasted. *John Keylock collection*

Below: Another 1911 view of Llanymynech. *T. R. Perkins collection*

Top: **Two railway companies, three trains and vintage stock on all of them.** *T. R. Perkins collection*

Middle: **The south end of Llanymynech station, looking towards Welshpool in 1932. The SMLR makes a double connection to the GWR from the left and then the Nantmawr branch immediately strikes off to the right.** *WEH-LYN collection*

Left: **By 1946 the track layout had been rationalised, with the SMLR connection made single with a single-blade trap point to protect the main line.** *Author's collection*

3

The Shropshire Railways

The dissolution of the PSNWR company was a protracted and complicated affair, not completed until 1 November 1895. Young found no interest from any of the railway companies in taking on the PSNWR. Of the most likely and feasible candidates, the GWR and LNWR maintained their monopoly on Shrewsbury traffic as long as it remained closed and therefore had no interest in it. The Cambrian, which had already secured control of the Nantmawr traffic, might have been persuaded to take on its own independent route to Shrewsbury but had no funds with which to do so. A way out of the impasse would be to form a new company to take over the old.

Some time in 1887, Sir Richard Dansey Green Price Bt, James Inman and John Parson Smith came forward to do just that, having their solicitors announce that they would be depositing a bill to incorporate the Shropshire Railways in December of that year. As presented, the bill sought powers to take over the PSNWR, to vary the terms of sale as defined in the 1881 winding-up act, to make new railways, for running powers on the Great Western Railway between Hodnet and Market Drayton on the Wellington and Market Drayton line, which would give access to the North Staffordshire Railway at Silverdale Junction, and all of the North Staffordshire and Cambrian systems, and to maintain the substantial part of the Market Drayton line as a separate undertaking with separate capital and accounts.

The proposed new railways were two short lines in Shrewsbury, the first to raise the existing line above the flood plain, with the consequential effect of easing the gradient, the other to have the effect of making a triangular junction with the

loop line in order that trains to and from the east could use the station without reversing. The other two lines revived the old SPJR target of Market Drayton and Stoke-on-Trent, these to be double track. Railway No 4, between Hodnet and Market Drayton, would run parallel to the existing GWR route between those places but would not be required if the running powers were granted. A proposal to build a 'direct' route between Oswestry and Kinnerley was dropped before the bill reached the select committees. During a series of meetings held to promote the bill some £3,500 was raised in contributions towards its expenses.

Price was a landowner from Radnorshire who had bought property near Shrewsbury some five years previously and who was a director of the Golden Valley and the Kington & Eardisley Railways, neither of them notable successes. Inman lived in Paris and was alleged to be rich and the owner of property in Wolverhampton. At the time of the select committee hearings, Price had not met him, and said that it was Young who had proposed his involvement. Smith was a successful Shrewsbury merchant, having been goods manager of the Shropshire Union Canal for 14 years and lessee of the Nantmawr, the Bellyn Bank and Criggion quarries. Price and Smith first took an interest in the PSNWR in 1886.

Subject to Parliamentary approval, they had made a formal agreement of sale with Young on 14 March 1888, agreeing to

Cambrian Railways 0-6-0 No 15 and its short train stand at Llanymynech, bound for Llanyblodwell, c1904.
T. R. Perkins collection

Above: **On the Criggion branch, Melverley river bridge shortly before it collapsed. Anyone who would climb on to a bridge in this condition was either brave or foolhardy.** *E. L. Morton*

Left: **Crew Green distant signal was photographed on 5 August 1904; T. R. Perkins holds the lever.** *F. E. Fox-Davies*

unnecessary with respect to or for the purposes of either local traffic or through traffic ... they are most objectionable as they will deprive your petitioners of traffic .... The proposed railways have been badly selected and designed.' They made a concerted effort to demolish the promoters' case, *inter alia* objecting that the proposed bridge over the Wellington line would prevent them widening it in the future. It was revealed that existing road bridges over the line in the same locality had the same clearances as those proposed for the SR structure. They also believed that no satisfactory financial arrangements had been made to acquire the PSNWR or the new works and called on the committee to inquire into the source and nature of the deposit lodged with the bill.

The Earl of Bradford, who owned land around Knockin, Nesscliffe and Kinnerley, confirmed what he had said in 1881, that the PSNWR had not paid for land valued at about £10,000 but he wanted the railway to be resuscitated and was now prepared to take shares in the new company in part settlement.

The Mayor of Shrewsbury, Vincent Crump, in expressing support, and that of the town, for the railway said he was 'anxious to see it opened or else I should not have come to London. I have not been here since the exhibition of 1851, and I shall not come again if I can help it.'

Thomas Southam, an alderman, said that the PSNWR had failed due to its management: 'It was financed and worked by one man – a Mr France – a very energetic, but a very obstinate man I may say, and he persisted in making the Llanymynech [line] first instead of making the potteries line first.' He added that before the line was closed the rolling stock had got into a

pay 'such an amount of fully paid-up stock in the Shrewsbury Separate Undertaking of the Shropshire company as would enable the liquidator to pay in such stock at the par value thereof the maximum percentages mentioned in ... the winding-up act'. The purchase price was to be £12,300 in cash plus £286,432 3s 4d in stock.

The select committee hearings were held in the House of Lords on 26 and 27 April 1888, and on 23-25 July in the Commons. The LNWR and GWR made their objection jointly, saying that the proposed railways were 'wholly uncalled for and

poor state of repair and people refused to travel by it. During one of his four periods in the mayoralty, c1866/7, he had been 'memorialised' to petition the BoT about the state of the trains.

For the promoters, Price explained the significance of the Market Drayton line, saying that the Nantmawr limestone was of high quality and in demand for fluxing in iron making at works in Hodnet and Hanley; the through route via Market Drayton would be five or six miles shorter. If the Criggion quarries were developed and their stone made available in Staffordshire it would compete well with Clee Hill stone from south Shropshire, saving 2s per ton in transport alone. One of the scheme's supporters was a senior partner in BS, financiers of the PSNWR.

When questioned by the GWR's barrister, Price had to admit that the railway would have to earn £35,000 per annum in order to make a 5% return on the proposed £350,000 capital. The PSNWR's best year had been 1875, when £13,552 was earned to make a loss of £2,481.

Price's assertion that the £40,000 needed to fund the PSNWR's restoration to traffic would be funded by a first charge on the undertaking, by debentures, was met with a certain incredulity. The Bank of Scotland was the source, it transpired, of a £13,056 6s 3d loan to the promoters that funded the Parliamentary deposit.

Young explained that he had received assents to the proposal to issue SR stock as compensation for PSNWR shares and debentures to the value of £1,090,000. There had been one dissenter with a holding of £217 debenture stock, but it would be impossible to get a 100% response because some holders had died or moved without notifying a change of address.

John Russell, the engineer, went over the estimates. The PSNWR main line would cost £27,000, the Breidden branch £11,000, and the Llanyblodwell branch £3,000, to bring them

Right: **The road underbridge between Criggion station and the quarries.** *T. R. Perkins collection*

Below: **Llanymynech is dominated by an outcrop of limestone. In this view from the south the Cambrian line is out of sight to the right, and the Nantmawr/Llanfyllin line runs in the shallow cutting just beyond the river.** *Author's collection*

up to passenger-carrying standards. For the new works, the alterations at Shrewsbury were estimated to cost £30,255 and the Market Drayton line £238,702. There was no provision in the estimates for rolling stock.

Despite the best efforts of the LNWR and the GWR the Lords passed the bill. In the House of Commons much the same ground was gone over again, with mostly the same witnesses although with the addition of support from the local MPs.

After an adjournment, the Commons committee declared that it was not prepared to grant running powers over the GWR, thus forcing the SR to undertake to build its seven-mile long railway No 4. The SR gave way on the question of the spans of the overbridges over the Wellington line and the GWR's Market Drayton line and obtained agreement over the installation of a junction between railway No 4 and the GWR.

These notes on the select committees are of necessity condensed, as the verbatim record required nearly 300 printed pages. The point is, the case for the SR was, like that for the PSNWR, extremely ill-founded. With regard to the SR, the PSNWR's stockholders were blinded by the original £1.3 million expenditure and the settlement requirements of the 1881 act to believe that they had an asset that had a realisable value,

whereas in fact it was, until the SR came on the scene, worthless. Apart from the Nantmawr branch the railway was disused and earning nothing.

The SR promoters were also blinded by the original £1.3 million expenditure and thought they could acquire it on the cheap. The 1881 act's settlement requirements made the capital valuation too high, bearing in mind that the railway would need to earn more than twice what the PSNWR earned to produce a satisfactory return for the stockholders. Even with reliable stone traffic there was no reason to expect that the overall business would more than double. The promoters should have been prepared to stand their ground and negotiate the settlement down. It would have been harder, but the PSNWR investors had no alternative. Then the railway might have been viable.

The promoters then lumbered themselves with the Market Drayton line, and double track at that, arguing that it was

essential if they were to get investors' support for reviving the bankrupt PSNWR. Together with the PSNWR it was touted as an alternative through route, via Llanymynech, Oswestry and Mold, from the Midlands to North Wales. That the promoters were not prepared to make a public share issue before approaching the financiers or to invest substantial sums of their own money surely demonstrates the inherent weakness of the scheme. Hindsight is a very precise science.

The act received the royal assent on 7 August 1888. The company was incorporated and the provisional agreement with Young confirmed. The PSNWR together with railways Nos 1 and 2 and a small part of railway No 3 were incorporated into the 'Shrewsbury Separate Undertaking', with £350,000 capital, the remainder into the 'Market Drayton separate undertaking', with £300,000 capital. For each of the undertakings £100,000 was allowed to be borrowed. The first directors were Price,

Inman and Smith together with a Richard Taylor and two others suitably qualified with a holding of £500 of stock in either undertaking. Taylor was a Shrewsbury JP.

The existence of the SR act did nothing to speed up the transfer of the PSNWR and it was 12 October 1888 before the SR directors met for the first time. After Price had been appointed chairman topics discussed included claims in respect of railway land that had not been paid for. Settling these claims was to be a priority 'with the least possible expenditure of cash'.

The name of William Greer Barcroft was submitted and accepted as a director. He was a shareholder in the Mold & Denbigh Junction Railway who lived at Mold, was retired and would, the board was informed, 'be able to devote as much time as might be required'.

The original directors were introduced by Young to Cutbill, Son & de Lungo, contractors and financiers. On 30 July 1888, CSdL had agreed to provide the permanent Parliamentary deposit of £13,056 6s 3d in 2¾% consols (long-term fixed-rate government stock), allowing the Bank of Scotland's temporary loan to be redeemed. The agreement required the company to make the interest up to 5%. Further, in return for providing the deposit CSdL was to have the option of taking cash contracts to build either or both of the Market Drayton or Shrewsbury lines. If, within two years, the loan had not been repaid or construction of the undertakings had not been started then the directors would, at their own expense, apply to Parliament for an abandonment bill. CSdL agreed to advance £5,000 to be used to settle land claims and other preliminary expenses on 13 December 1888, and on 2 August 1889 tendered to reconstruct the PSNWR from Shrewsbury Abbey for £70,000, comprising £16,666 in shares at 60%, £10,000; old rails, £5,800; cash, £54,200 and was accepted subject to contract.

On 19 February 1889 the SR board agreed to ask Young for a further six months to complete the PSNWR purchase. In August, the court order intended to authorise it was not satisfactory because the SR would only be given possession of the PSNWR instead of ownership, a position that would have left the SR unable to issue debentures.

By 30 August the order had been amended, apparently made on 17 July, and a breakdown of the money needed to reconstruct the railway produced (Table 1). The issue of £275,685 0s 9d stock and £5,000 debentures was required for the SR to fulfil the requirements of the 1881 act.

Table 1

Finance requirement for Shropshire Railways

Cash for works	£54,200 0s 0d
Costs of 1881 act and liquidation expenses	£5,514 8s 5d
Costs of 1888 act	£2,401 7s 2d
Land claims	£3,721 9s 9d
Cash per order	£2,031 15s 4d
Law and engineering expenses	£4,000 0s 0d
Establishment charges	£1,000 0s 0d
Interest on construction	£5,000 0s 0d
	£77,869 0s 8d

Previously, on 24 August 1888, apparently at Young's instigation, an auction of PSNWR stock was held in Shrewsbury. According to T. R. Perkins, who was present (see Bibliography), four locomotives, *Bradford*, *Powis*, *Hope* and *Tanat*, realised £305, £210, £200 and £85 respectively, while the 200-odd wagons fetched 'varying prices according to their dilapidation'. Why the sale took place at this time is open to question.

By March 1890 Price was negotiating with Whadcoat Bros & Co Ltd, described as bankers and contractors of public works. During that month Inman had met PSNWR stock-holders and had asked *them* if they would buy SR debentures to finance the railway's reconstruction. When it had become clear that that this was not a fruitful source of enquiry the directors resolved, on 30 April 1890, 'that the chairman be authorised to negotiate an agreement with Messrs Whadcoat Bros & Co Ltd for taking the debenture capital and finding money to pay for the reconstruction and reopening of the line between Shrewsbury and Llanymynech and paying out the liquidator and satisfying the landowners and for legal, engineering and directorial expenses ...'

An agreement that Whadcoats would pay £79,500 to the SR within 14 days of the company making a contract with a 'reputable' contractor was accepted by the board on 23 May 1890 and sealed on 3 June. To save money the original iron rails were to be re-used rather than be replaced by steel.

CSdL's terms for undertaking the construction contract proved to be unacceptable and the board resolved on 25 July 1890 to award the contract to Charles Chambers for a price not exceeding £64,000: £44,000 payable in cash, the balance in shares. Price must have been the agent for involving Chambers as both had connections with the Golden Valley Railway. The contract was approved on 1 August and had been executed by 19 August when the directors gave authority to Chambers to take possession of the

The Llanfyllin branch junction, looking towards the Wern overbridges and Llanymynech. The additional supports required by the canal aqueduct can be seen.
T. R. Perkins collection

The first crossing of the Afon Tanat by the Nantmawr branch was at Carreghofa. The bridge is seen with handrails installed by the Cambrian after the TVLR opened in 1904 and a passenger service was operated between Llanymynech and Blodwell Junction.
T. R. Perkins collection

property. Chambers expected the reconstruction to take 14 months. The deposit financed by CSdL remained in place and that company was not reimbursed.

Eventually, the PSNWR was transferred to the SR. Young had been ordered to seal the conveyance on 15 July 1890 and the indenture was made on 6 August but the company was still not wound up. Although the land claims were settled straight away (the releases were dated between 28 July and 12 August), it was not until the autumn that Young distributed SR stock to the PSNWR stockholders; the transfer register was brought into use on 8 October 1890. In 1890/1, the Railway & Public Companies Finance Association disposed of £18,100 of stock, including £7,100 to Chambers and £5,000 to Whadcoat family members. The Whadcoat brothers increased their influence by making other acquisitions during the next two years. The London Financial Association Ltd made both disposals and acquisitions. Taylor acquired £400 of stock and Smith and Price £250 each.

Arising from the imminent start of works the Midland Wagon Works was asked to remove its property from the SR's land to avoid impeding the contractor. The 1888 auction of rolling stock notwithstanding, two locomotives remained at Shrewsbury, perhaps the sale had fallen through; £160 was offered for them but the board required £200 on 10 September 1890. They were still there in October but nothing more was said about them.

Over the next 12 months a good part of the reconstruction was carried out, Russell reporting on 1 April 1891 that nearly all the excavations and embankments were almost completed, 12 bridges were 'practically completed', the abutments built and girders were in place on two others and the arches were turned on another two; the Shrawardine bridge re-decking was nearly complete; three fifths of the 22 miles of railway and sidings had been resleepered with new bolts and spikes and had been reballasted. About 9,000 sleepers, a large amount of permanent way and other materials, including new girders for three bridges, were on site ready to be used. He had previously reported that five miles of new fencing had been erected and ten miles of hedges laid. Russell produced his report on the work required at the stations on 21 May 1891, but it is unlikely that much of this work, if any, was done.

The relationship with Chambers had got off to a good start but in December 1890 he had been asked to reduce the amount of his monthly certificate. He replied that he could not do so as he had already entered into contracts for the supply of services and materials. At the end of that month £21,300 of work had

been certified. When Russell calculated the amount due on certificate No 6, worth £4,100 in March 1891 he reduced the prices payable against the contract; the issue then went to arbitration, and the award was made against the company. Chambers issued a writ for £3,000 on 13 May although the company had said that it accepted the arbitration award. When the company sent the stock certificates to which Chambers was entitled without the money due on 9 June Chambers' solicitor returned them. When work stopped in July 1891 Chambers had undertaken work with a certified value of £40,000.

Whadcoats acted as banker, releasing money on receipt and approval of Russell's certificates and other requests. The company issued mortgage debenture bonds in exchange for the money. When the cheque was received Chambers would be paid. There were further problems during 1890, with Whadcoats complaining that the company was failing to comply with the terms of the 3 June agreement. Two more agreements were made, on 1 August and 10 December 1890.

The rapport between the company and financier further deteriorated after January 1891, when interest due on debentures was not paid, perhaps hardly surprisingly as the company had no revenue. There was, of course, £5,000 in the budget for interest and Whadcoats was supposed to give this to the company for the company to pay some of it back to Whadcoats. The revenue from stocks sold to the public by the company, £3,701 2s by June 1890, was paid to Whadcoats and an appropriate value of bonds returned for cancellation.

There was not always unity amongst the directors, with Inman resigning on 13 December 1890. Although a mysterious figure at the time of the Parliamentary hearings, he had attended all the board meetings until 25 October 1890. He had objected to the contract being given to Chambers and his departure had been in the offing for some months, with his solicitor writing to the board concerning his expenses and other claims while he was still attending meetings. Richard Edmondson, who had been appointed to the board on 23 May 1890, objected to the change in Chambers' rates whilst maintaining his directorship. Clement Southam replaced Inman on 3 February 1891, but resigned on 24 April.

In February 1891, Price submitted his resignation because he had taken a post with the Local Government Board. However, on submission of an undertaking that the company's meetings would be held in the evening and that he would not let his involvement interfere with his public office the board sanctioned his continuing with the SR, allowing him to withdraw his resignation on 6 March. On 25 November 1891, when the writing was clearly on the wall, the directors decided to apportion £1,737 10s standing to their credit for expenses: Price, Smith and Taylor £347 10s each, Barcroft £322 10s; Inman £276 5s, and Edmondson £96 5s.

Despite the need to focus on raising money and getting the works completed the directors could not ignore the opportunities to consider expansion. In October 1890, Price and Russell were to examine, at the request of landowners and residents, the possibility of an extension to serve the Tanat Valley, the board considering that an extension to Llangynog would be in the company's interest. Russell, at the same time, had been asked to assess the works needed to make the Breidden branch fit for goods traffic. His estimate was £9,900, and expenditure on fencing it, £5, was approved in December 1890.

Russell was in constant dialogue with the board over money owed to him. In 1890 he was still due fees and expenses arising from the 1888 act. By 18 March 1891 he was owed £2,625; at the next meeting he was paid £250 from the Market Drayton account, £50 from the London account and £50 from the Shrewsbury account.

Relationships with the neighbouring railway companies were good. In November 1890 a draft agreement with the Cambrian covered a connection between the Nantmawr branch and the Cambrian's Llanfyllin line and, within six months of powers being obtained, entering into an agreement 'for the working in perpetuity of your railway … less the Breidden branch'. The SR's readiness in having another railway work its services may explain the disposal of the PSNWR locomotives. The Cambrian was also asked to build a siding on the Nantmawr branch for Lord Bradford at Llanddu, the cost to be set against tolls due to the SR. Correspondence with the joint lines over a connection at or near Red Hill was amicable although not as far as agreeing to give access to the joint station.

Bills to apply for an extension of time and 'general powers' were deposited in December 1890. These were the cause of complaints by Whadcoats, who should have been consulted under the terms of their agreement with the company. The British Linen Bank agreed to fund the temporary deposit on payment of 200 guineas commission.

In a measure to appease Whadcoats after the January 1891 debenture interest went unpaid, the company gave them a lien on all money or stock due to the company from the liquidator as security for the interest, and the interest on that. Prospectuses for 5% 'perpetual first debenture stock' were issued on 19 January and 6 April 1891. This stock, the would-be applicants were informed, was a first charge on the Shrewsbury Separate Undertaking and the interest was payable in priority to dividends on the ordinary stock. Whadcoats agreed to support the prospectuses on what appear to be their standard terms; any advance was to be repaid within six months together with 10% interest and 5% commission. The January prospectus raised only £11,400. It, unless there was more than one issued on that date, was headed 'special prospectus for the proprietors of the London & North Western, Great Western, North Stafford and Cambrian Railways companies' in red. Whether targeting stockholders of the SR's neighbours was a ruse to try to persuade those companies' shareholders that *those companies* should also invest in the SR is not clear.

Various stockholdings became a concern for the board during 1891, initially when they realised that they did not hold the qualifying shareholding as specified by the 1888 act. Russell and the solicitors were to surrender stock issued to them as surety and receive the cash. Price and Smith had £250 each, Edmondson £500, and Taylor £400. On 17 April 1891, the board was notified that Whadcoats had transferred 447 of its mortgage debenture bonds to John Henry Whadcoat and 362 to William Edward Whadcoat, as security for advances of £21,000 and £15,946 4s 0d respectively, to the Whadcoat company. The

Above: **The second Afon Tanat crossing was nearer Llanyblodwell. This photograph shows the bridge pre-1904.**
T. R. Perkins collection

Left: **In this post-1904 view it is probably the Perkins brothers posing for the camera.**
T. R. Perkins collection

board was unnerved by this and ordered that it must be informed before any future transfers were registered. The parties to a transfer of £65,157 ordinary shares were not identified when its registration was recorded on 17 October but the new owners were the Whadcoats.

Construction stopped on 15 July 1891, when Chambers withdrew his men after Whadcoats ceased funding the SR. Russell was given permission to remove his agent from the site on 17 October 1891; he calculated that Chambers had completed 54% of the works. The company and Chambers commenced proceedings against Whadcoats.

Whadcoats was in default of the contract, the directors declared on 16 July 1891, when they offered to advance £209 13s 6d personally to pay the debenture interest due on 1 July. A circular that had been sent to SR stockholders by the Railways & Public Finance Association on 13 July was read on this date. It had been signed by R. Ullmer, Whadcoats' company secretary, so must be presumed to be an attack on the railway board.

The Shropshire Railways Act 1891 received the royal assent on 21 July. Rather than petitioning against the bill, CSdL had tried to obtain an injunction to prevent it proceeding, but its application was refused as being beyond the court's remit. The act extended the compulsory purchase powers until 7 August 1893 and the time for completion until 7 August 1896. New share capital of £75,000, £16,600 additional borrowing on the original capital, and £25,000 borrowing on the new capital were authorised. Voting rights, omitted from the 1888 act, were defined. The 'general powers' bill failed because the company was unable to raise funds for its deposit; its objects included a Tanat Valley extension.

On the application of W. E. Whadcoat on 31 July 1891, the company was placed in receivership because of the unpaid interest, Richard Rabbidge being appointed receiver on 11 November 1891. Several dilapidated cottages, including those at Wern Las and Kinnerley, were repaired to make them lettable and to provide Rabbidge with an income with which he could administer the company.

Receivership was arguably the least of the SR's problems for by the end of the year it was involved in no fewer than five legal actions. The company and Chambers had sued Whadcoats and been counter-sued; a Mr Webb, Chambers' clerk, and Inman had both issued writs against the company and then there was 'Whadcoats libel action'. CSdL had also issued a writ over the construction contract earlier in 1891 and during 1892 the London Financial Association issued a writ for reasons unspecified.

The SR had claimed that the contract with Whadcoats was null and void because it had been broken by them; Whadcoats counterclaimed £20,000 damages: they had not been issued with any 'A' class debentures, presumably requiring the majority of all classes. The libel action arose from the company's half-year report published in December 1891 which accused Whadcoats of manipulating the stock to secure more influence. The transfer of bonds to the Whadcoats individually and the subsequent purchase of £65,157 ordinary shares by them had been done in such a way as to maximise the number of votes available to them. If they were able to get a place, or places, on the board, the board suggested, they would be in a position to stop the law suit brought against them by the company. Inman was pursuing a refund of the 1888 Parliamentary deposit to which he had contributed, an activity that was to engage him for a good number of years.

Blodwell Junction, Llanyblodwell before the TVLR opened in 1904. The original building is deteriorating while the Cambrian has erected a new building, on the left, for its own purposes.
T. R. Perkins collection

Russell was ordered to prepare plans for the Market Drayton line on 28 November 1891, when shares were issued to Price, Smith and Taylor, 50 each, Russell, two, and several others, one each.

After construction work came to an end the SR went into limbo, the frequency of board meetings reducing considerably. There were still matters requiring the board's attention that had consequences for the SR's future, apart from instructing Russell to cease planning work on the Market Drayton extension.

The Nantmawr branch was still nominally active under Cambrian control and Russell was instructed to inspect it. The Reverend T. B. Foulkes, writing from Llanyblodwel vicarage in May 1892, complained to the BoT about the dangerous condition of the SR's bridges in the area and the Oswestry Highways Board observed that the fences were in poor condition, too. The SR resolved to accept the Cambrian's offer to commute the toll on the 60ch of the Nantmawr branch used by Llanfyllin branch trains provided that any agreement did not put the SR under any liability regarding signalling, and did not inhibit the SR from using the branch without paying tolls to the Cambrian. These actions were taken on 11 October 1892.

Progress of a sort came in January 1893, with the making of two supplemental agreements with Whadcoats. For Price it came, literally at a price, his worst imaginings, for the Whadcoats had gained control of the SR. The board met on 11 February 1893 and Price and Barcroft were joined as directors by the Whadcoat brothers and Ullmer. John Henry Whadcoat was elected 'permanent chairman' and was to find a new office for the company in London. That was Price's last meeting. On 13 July the transfer of his Market Drayton shares to William Edward Whadcoat was registered and the secretary reported that he had written to Price to tell him that he was no longer a director of that undertaking and that his successor had been appointed. Only Barcroft and Smith remained from the old regime although Smith did not attend meetings for a while.

Even with the change in control and the company still in receivership, the directors' focus remained unchanged, reopening the PSNWR and building the Market Drayton line. A £2 call was made on the latter's shares in July 1893. Perhaps some part of the PSNWR was fit for traffic, or nearly so, for on 22 July 1893 the chairman was authorised to 'agree terms for Mr Griffiths to convey goods and minerals on the line'.

The relationship with Chambers deteriorated further and on 22 July 1893 he was given three weeks' notice to resume work and threatened with the consequences if there were any problems arising from his activities or lack of them. A week later he was told not to use the company's name in any existing or future action. He was later seen surveying on the Nantmawr branch; a solicitor was to be retained to advise if he was trespassing. When Llanymynech station was found to be locked up with a notice reading 'contractors office' attached to it the directors were even less happy. Whatever he was doing, Chambers was not making any progress on the works. By 30 August the board wanted to replace him but could not make contact with Russell to get obtain information to enable a contractor to tender. A new engineer, who would give credit, was required.

The secretary, E. B. Smith received short shrift from the board on 30 August 1893. Not having been paid, the details were not recorded, he took action against the company, and was awarded judgment in his favour. Hearing this, the board decided to pay him £12 for his services until 30 September and sacked him with immediate effect. Ullmer became secretary on 6 November, his place on the board being taken by James Irvine.

The legal issues did not go away and in November 1892 and

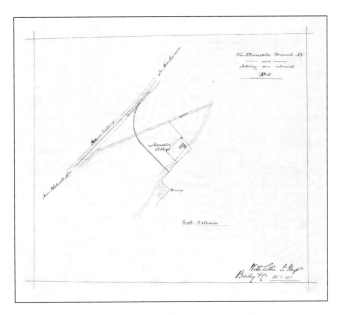

A sketch showing the proposed siding required by the Earl of Bradford at Llanddu, October 1877. *National Archives*

1893, CSdL deposited two Parliamentary bills to try to regain control of the SR deposit. Under the terms of the 1892 bill, the North Salop Railway would take ownership of the Market Drayton undertaking and control of the Shrewsbury undertaking, charging the SR interest on the cost of completing it. Failing with this, the following year an abandonment bill was promoted. The company petitioned against the bill and on 4 May 1894 the House of Lords select committee found that 'the promoters have not made out their case, and the bill should not proceed'. In the meantime, on 30 August 1893, a bill for costs of £29 0s 8d, was received in a case 're Berrington', the first the board knew of it. It was not mentioned again.

Russell was replaced by Ridley & Moss on 6 November 1893, 'the position of the company having been fully explained'. The claims for £3,398 for his work on the Shropshire Separate Undertaking and £42 in respect of the Market Drayton Separate Undertaking were deferred. Settlement was reached in January 1895 for a total of £4,000; possibly £1,000 of this was in cash provided by Whadcoats, the remainder was 1891 debentures.

The state of the infrastructure, being unfinished, was regularly before the board's attention. On 11 April 1894 alone there were letters from Shropshire County Council, about road approaches and bridges, the joint railways, about the bridge over the Hereford line; and the Shropshire Union Canal and about the leaking aqueduct over the Nantmawr branch. The repair bill of £5 16s 1d for the latter was passed to the receiver.

W. E. Whadcoat resigned from the board on 11 April 1894. Smith, present for the first time since the Whadcoat take-over, was required to read the minutes for the meetings that he had missed. J. H. Whadcoat resigned on 7 January 1895 and it may be relevant that £36,363 of 1891 debentures were registered to him the next day. He was replaced by George Bush, a director of the Devon & Somerset Railway, while Irvine was elected chairman. Surely someone was indulging in some wishful thinking when they suggested that the Whadcoat brothers should be authorised to have free lifetime passes on the SR, its branches and extensions? Still dealing with the board, Smith resigned on 27 February 1895 and was replaced by Edward Bertie Haselden shortly afterwards.

Debentures of 1891 to the value of £36,364 acquired by W. E. Whadcoat in 1895/6 were not his brother's as *his* entire holding of £41,364 was transferred to Emma Whadcoat a few weeks later, and she was to transfer most of it back in 1900.

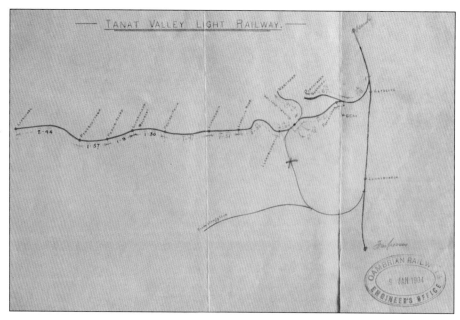

The Cambrian Railways' distance diagram of the TVLR produced four days after the line had been opened. 'Lord Bradford's curve' between the Nantmawr branch and the TVLR has been pencilled in. *National Archives*

Notable names amongst the holders of the debentures were Samuel Morton Peto, the contractor with £1,000, John Plimsoll Brocklebank, of the shipping line, a third share in £7,403; the Mid Wales Railway, £31, and the Cambrian Railways, £374. An insignificant holding of only £7 registered on 19 April 1895 is only of interest because its owner, Frederick Pring Robjent, became a director of the Festiniog Railway Company in 1908.

In a move that sounds a bit suspect given that the company was in receivership, it was agreed on 19 June 1894 that the rent on a cottage at Kinnerley should be paid directly to J. H. Whadcoat 'in reduction of indebtedness by company to him'.

By the start of 1895 it looked as though there was progress towards getting the railway reopened. Despite a fresh contract having been made between Whadcoats and Chambers in 1894, a provisional contract was made with W. E. Clayton-Smith to complete the works. The Whadcoat brothers, acting separately, were appointed trustees to each of the parties to oversee it. Debenture holders had been asked, and most had agreed, to capitalise their interest payments until 1897. Young was being urged to wind up the PSNWR and a new prospectus was about to be issued.

There is no obvious explanation for Young's prevarication over the liquidation; perhaps he was able to claim fees or expenses as long as it lasted. The SR's prompting had some effect for Young applied to complete the liquidation on 11 February 1895. Most of the transactions in his certified accounts were dated 1890/1, and the most recent, concerning a claim in respect of land was in 1893, so the work cannot have taxed him for some time.

When the board met on 27 February 1895 it was mainly to discuss the prospectus. The document had been printed but it needed final approval. When the question arose of whether the fact of the company being in receivership should be mentioned, the solicitors' and counsel's opinions were sought. It was approved for publication on 16 March and issued on 25 March.

By 29 March any idea that the SR had a future had collapsed. Buried amongst the financial news, that day's *Times* contained the simple yet disastrous announcement that 'The company is said to be in the hands of a receiver, owing to default on its first mortgage debenture stock. If this allegation is true the fact should have been mentioned in the prospectus lately issued ...' During a meeting held that day which started at the company's London office and transferred to its solicitors, the board resolved to send a letter to the *Pall Mall Gazette*, which had also noticed the deficiency, and to copy it to the *Times*.

In its 30 March 1895 issue the *Times* railed: 'The only portion of this communication which is of interest to us ... is the admission that "it is true that a receiver of the tolls and revenue, not of the capital issues, was appointed some time since in the interests of the holders of debentures ..."' The paper continued: 'This being the case, we have no hesitation in saying that the

fact now admitted should have been stated ... we are surprised that men of business should have imagined ... that any other course should have been right or expedient. The fact alleged ... that the receivership will end on the payment of a not very large sum has nothing to do with the case, and the assertion that a receiver and a liquidator are not identical in function is equally irrelevant. The directors ought to have foreseen that the actual position ... was certain to be discovered very speedily, and that the discovery could not fail to impress intending investors unfavourably. Possibly they may have been technically correct in their idea that the fact referred to need not be disclosed. Their lawyer, it appears, advised them in this sense; but even supposing their view of the strict letter of the law can be defended, the board would have been wiser ... if they had openly stated the real position of the company. Lawyers are good servants, but bad masters ...'

The writer, 'a well-informed source', of a letter published anonymously on 2 April made it worse, if such were possible, by remarking: 'I should have thought it would have been even more interesting to know what the receiver receives' and summarised the railway's history. His final remark, on the railway's partial reconstruction and abandonment, concluding as it did 'Whether the contractor was paid I cannot say' leads this writer to speculate that Chambers was the culprit. If that was not enough, the company's bankers, the Capital & Counties Bank, then declared that it did not know that the company was in receivership.

At another meeting, held on 5 April 1895, the board decided that no allotment of debentures should take place and that any money received should be refunded. Ullmer was instructed to inform the *Times* accordingly. In publishing his letter on 6 April the paper commented: 'We are glad to receive the following letter ... the course announced being the only proper one in the circumstances.'

So far as the board was concerned nothing more could be done. The receiver continued to administer the dormant company and railway. Irvine, Bush and Haselden submitted their resignations before the year's end but they remained in office technically, because the resignations had not been accepted. From 1897, the railway's entry in the BoT returns was marked: 'There are neither directors nor officers to make the return.'

It was not until 6 June 1900 that the board next met, the impetus being the need to approve an agreement made by Rabbidge for the Cambrian to lease the Nantmawr branch for

99 years, which had been signed on 1 May 1900. The Cambrian guaranteed a minimum annual payment of £550 and also agreed to pay £5 annually for an easement to make a connection with the Nantmawr branch and its Llanfyllin line, and a £150 annual rental for the use of the part of the Nantmawr branch by Llanfyllin trains. Irvine, Barcroft and Bush attended the meeting as directors. The resignations were accepted and then Irvine and Bush were re-elected. Both J. H. and W. E. Whadcoat were elected, the former in place of Haselden. J. H. Whadcoat was elected chairman and proposed as receiver and manager subject to Rabbidge resigning. On J. H. Whadcoat's proposal, it was agreed to exchange debenture bonds for debenture certificates, for the benefit of the Whadcoat brothers of course; bonds to the value of £16,775 were not converted until 7 January 1907. A meeting of stockholders was called to ratify the Cambrian agreement; the revenue would be allocated to the bondholders, averaging a 1½% return.

The Cambrian had wanted the agreement as a part of the development of the long-awaited Tanat Valley Railway. The Tanat Valley Light Railway Order had been made on 4 January 1899, promoted by an independent company with the Cambrian's support. Thanks to the influence of the Earl of Bradford, who had maintained a long correspondence with the BoT concerning the SR, 19 chains of the Nantmawr branch at Llanyblodwell were incorporated into the TVLR's route to Oswestry. However, the Cambrian charged the TVLR not only the capital cost of bringing its mineral line from Llynclys to Porthywaen up to passenger train standards, but also the cost applicable to improving the Nantmawr branch to Llanymynech. An annual £250 payment towards the Cambrian's £550 was also charged for its use. Crucially, the authorised south-to-west curve, which would have enabled direct access between the TVLR and Llanymynech, was not made so the TVLR had to pay for a section of railway that its Cambrian-operated trains used very little. The TVLR was opened on 5 January 1904, when Llanyblodwell station became Blodwell Junction, a new station on the TVLR taking the old name. Until 1913 there was a limited service between the TVLR and Llanymynech which required either a shunt or a change of trains at Blodwell Junction.

The unbuilt curve, railway No 2, generated considerable correspondence and legal activity over the years. In correspondence it was usually referred to as 'Lord Bradford's curve'. Whether it was not built because the TVLR had insufficient funds or because the Cambrian discouraged its construction is not known. In later years the Cambrian certainly did not want it to be built because it would have completed a triangular junction and each point of the triangle would have required signalling and a manned signalbox.

At around this time the Nantmawr quarry lease was taken on by the Lilleshall Company Ltd; a contract was made between the company and the Cambrian on 14 November 1899. Under Lilleshall's control the stone was taken to its iron and steel works at Oakengates, Shropshire, via Llanymynech and Oswestry, hardly the most direct of routes. Some of it was burned into lime in kilns located close to the incline foot. Close to the quarry a terrace of houses called Lilleshall Cottages still stands as testimony to the period of that company's operation.

The possibility that the SR might have a future was only hinted at when the board next met in 1906: 'Correspondence between the chairman and the managing director of the Kent & East Sussex Railway was discussed.' The KESR's managing director was none other than Holman Fred Stephens, an engineer based in Tonbridge, Kent, who was achieving a measure of notoriety for his interest in the management and construction of light railways. The directors agreed to offer the rails, chairs and

other ironwork for sale by tender and noted that the receiver had been running the estate at a small profit, accumulating a surplus of £3,471 18s since 1891. W. E. Whadcoat's death had been the trigger for the meeting, which took place on 22 November 1906; he was replaced by James Moorman.

Whadcoat and Barcroft visited the railway on 20 December 1906, finding that some of its property was in occupation by various parties without the payment of rent. At Shrewsbury, the Midland Railway Wagon Co was using a siding and had buried a rail stack under several tons of cinders and at Llanymynech they found that it was quite obvious that the Cambrian had been making use of a siding; the secretary was to try to agree rental terms with both parties. Before long both claims were placed with the solicitors – after more than ten years of inaction it took no time at all for the directors to enmesh the SR with the law. Travelling between Hanwood and Llanymynech by trolley they had found that the stations (sic) were in course of demolition, including one that was being let when they last visited, probably at least ten years previously.

During the day they met Stephens in Shrewsbury, leading to a decision not to sell the rails. Stephens had said that he expected to be able to make an offer to take over the railway and to work it as a light railway. Discussing the matter on 17 January 1907 the board agreed to ask Stephens to make an offer and that interest on the cost of reconstruction should form a first charge on new receipts or traffic. Agreeing to further expenditure, even if not theirs, seems rather foolhardy for a company as seriously in debt as the SR. On the same occasion Joseph Henderson was elected to the board to replace the recently deceased Irvine.

Stephens maintained contact with the board, writing on 22 March 1907 that he estimated that it would cost £32,000 to complete and equip the SR's main line for traffic. At a later date a further £8,000 was added in respect of the Criggion branch. On 15 April he wrote to ask for 'certain options to induce him to obtain powers'. Ullmer, still secretary, wrote on 9 May 1907: '... I am authorised ... to give you the option to purchase at par, by completing and opening the main line ... providing the rolling stock, working capital and other matters as per your estimate, £32,000 4½% stock if and when the same is authorised to be issued, such stock to rank in priority to the existing stock etc. of the company. The security for the interest on such stock to be the net traffic receipts of the main line when completed and opened, but exclusive of the existing revenue receipts which will continue to belong to the existing debenture holders.

'The company will do all in its power to assist your application for the light railway order and in the issue to you of the £32,000 stock when authorised.

'Providing you make the application in due form during this month and without delay proceed with the same, this option will remain in force for six months after the granting of the light railway order or up to the date of its rejection by the commissioners.

'In any event it is understood no charge or claim is to be made on this company for costs or expenses or services of any description.'

By this means the SR would retain ownership of the railway in the unlikely event that Stephens's proposed operation struck the proverbial pot of gold while apparently funding the reconstruction using the money raised from the issue of a new class of debentures. In practice, the debentures would be issued, not for cash but in exchange for work carried out, just as had happened with Chambers and the SR, and with France and the PSNWR. At the same time the debenture interest would be secured on the net revenue of the railway operation, something that would be beyond the control of the SR's directors.

KINNERLEY DEPOT AND THE BRANCHES

Left: **Looking west towards Llanymynech at the Criggion branch junction, 1911.** *F. E. Fox-Davies*

Below: **The locomotive shed at Kinnerley, which replaced the PSNWR sheds at Shrewsbury and Llanymynech, seen in 1911. The machine shop was located in the lean-to extension on the left.** *A. M. Davies collection*

Bottom: **A later view from the rear of the loco shed showing the windmill that drove a water pump.** *A. M. Davies collection*

Above: **Two of the ex-LNWR 0-6-0 coal engines on shed.**
WEH-LYN collection

Left: **An interior view of the machine shop, showing the belt drives, the forge and parts of locomotives lying around.**
A. M. Davies collection

Below: **Inside the shed, an ex-LSWR 0-6-0 is receiving attention alongside 0-4-2ST No 2 *Hecate*.** *A. M. Davies collection*

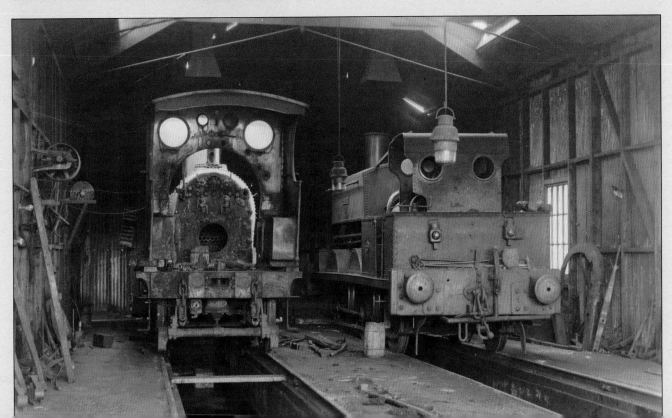

Top: The area around the shed became known amongst enthusiasts for the collection of ancient or dismantled locomotives lying around. Here, the boilers of two of the ex-LBSCR 0-6-0Ts are seen with *Hecate's* tank on the ground. *WEH-LYN collection*

Above: A shed scene in August 1926. From the left are No 9 *Daphne*, No 6 *Thisbe*, No 8 *Dido* and No 1 *Gazelle. H. C. Casserley*

Right: The materials might be different but even the Royal Engineers could not keep Kinnerley tidy, as seen in this 1958 view. The brick buildings, the high-level water tower and the Nissen hut are of military origin, as is the clerestory roof on the locomotive shed. *A. M. Davies*

CRIGGION BRANCH

Left: Along the branch, Chapel Lane had minimal facilities: a siding and a platform. *A. M. Davies*

Below: Melverley was noted for this unusual brick-arched road bridge where it appears that none of the arches had the same dimensions. The station building is visible through the centre arch. *A. M. Davies collection*

Bottom: The station and bridge are seen with an Army railcar on railtour duty in 1958. The bridge had a weight restriction and was demolished soon after the railway was closed. *A. M. Davies*

Above: **Melverley river bridge, *c*1912, after it had been rebuilt by Stephens and looking as though it incorporated some of France's iron beams taken from double-track structures that had been reduced in width.** *A. M. Davies*

Right: **Crew Green halt was only a basic timber platform with a small open waiting shelter. In this photograph it looks as though the track in the platform area has been de-turfed.** *Author's collection*

Below: **Breidden Hill dominates this view of Llandrinio Road station taken in September 1935.** *T. R. Perkins collection*

Above: **Criggion, 1958. The run-round loop was located on the Kinnerley side of the station which required terminating trains to set back before the locomotive could change ends.**
A. M. Davies

Left: **Michael Davies poses with the British Quarry Company's Sentinel locomotive at Criggion in October 1958.**
A. M. Davies

Below: **A 1922 Aveling & Porter convertible roller, probably owned by Montgomeryshire County Council, is parked up while on road mending duties alongside the Criggion mineral extension and Army Drewry railcar No 9105 in October 1958.**
A. M. Davies collection

NANTMAWR BRANCH

Above: **Blodwell Junction in 1963.** *A. M. Davies*

Below: **A reminder of the time when the Nantmawr branch was intended to be double track; the railway here was closed in 1925. Seen on 9 September 2007, the bridge carries the A495 road.** *Author*

Right: **Looking eastwards towards Porthywaen from the A495 overbridge at Blodwell Junction, 28 April 1982. The line to Nantmawr veers off to the left.** *Author*

Above: **At Llanddu Junction, wagons loaded with Nantmawr stone are propelled towards Blodwell Junction in 1964 by an Ivatt Class 2 2-6-0. The photographer was standing on the isolated section of the Tanat Valley Light Railway between the Nantmawr branch and the Cambrian's Porthywaen branch.** *A. M. Davies*

Left: **Looking towards Nantmawr on the branch, *c*1962. In 2007, the track remains *in situ* and the gates have been reinstated by members of the Cambrian Railways Society. Only some of the brickwork of the permanent way hut survives, but now invisible from this vantage point.** *A. M. Davies*

Below: **The end of the line, Nantmawr, *c*1961. The loading gantries and incline are out of sight behind the lime kilns. The loco is an ex-GWR 0-6-0PT.** *A. M. Davies*

The Shropshire & Montgomeryshire Light Railway

The first approach to the Board of Trade concerning the idea of reconstructing the Shropshire Railways as a light railway was made on 3 December 1906. Stephens wrote that he had 'had a proposal to reopen the line as a light railway'. He was informed that either the SR company, if it still existed, could apply for an order or 'a new body of promoters' could make an application for 'an order authorising the construction of a new railway over the same route and the compulsory acquisition of the land on which the derelict line was laid'.

The Board had actually missed the point that Stephens tried to make in his handwritten letter. His next was typewritten: 'If the railway was reconstructed could it be reopened following an inspection, ie using the original powers but meeting the requirements of a light railway?' The file containing the correspondence is annotated: 'Mr Stephens is still rather vague and does not say for whom he is acting.' The suggestion that he be sent a copy of Rich's 1880 report was rejected, the BoT replying that it had no information concerning the current state of the line on which to base an opinion, but would expect to receive detailed proposals that could be referred to the railway inspecting officers.

Just who made the proposal to reopen the SR as a light railway and how Stephens came to be involved is not known. An intermittent stream of articles in the railway press might well have played a part in raising the moribund railway's profile and thus bringing it to the attention of Stephens and his partners. It is equally possible that J. H. Whadcoat and Stephens might have met in Kent, for some time between 1895 and 1907 Whadcoat had moved to the Manor House at Bodiam, a locality served by Stephens' Kent & East Sussex Railway. Had the 1888 powers been deemed valid the promoters probably expected to have a claim on the act's deposit in respect of the Shrewsbury Separate Undertaking, not on the larger amount deposited for the Market Drayton undertaking. Following further consultations with the SR directors and the BoT, however, an application for a light railway order was submitted in May 1907. Stephens was named as a promoter, together with William Rigby, a contractor who had worked with him on other railways.

A public inquiry held in Shrewsbury on 9 July 1907 was well reported in local newspapers. Inman was the only objector, still trying to protect his interest in the Market Drayton Separate Undertaking deposit made in 1888. The company to be incorporated under the order was the North Shropshire Light Railway Co. In addition to the maximum of £40,000 required for the reconstruction, which would be secured on the SR's new debentures, the company would have £2,000 share capital.

It would be unable to issue more than £1,000 of this without the approval of the SR, a provision made to limit the amount of interest payable on the ordinary shares in favour of the debentures.

Stephens was reported as saying that he thought they would get on well with three engines, that six or seven carriages would carry a lot of people and that 'They would not want many trucks.' Rigby had tendered £17,480 to undertake the restoration. A Shropshire county councillor, Thomas Ward Green of Maesbrook, spoke in favour of the railway being reopened. Stephens' correspondence with him concerning the railway has survived; he was also to invest £100 in the SR's new debentures. John Kemble, the chairman of Llanymynech parish council, wrote that road maintenance around Kinnerley cost £19 per mile, because of the heavy use of road vehicles, whereas elsewhere in the area, well served by railways, the cost was only £13 per mile. Stephens made great play on the £5,000 turnover achieved by the PSNWR the year it closed; it was very good for a light railway and should be achievable here, and he could not understand why the railway had been closed in those circumstances. He appeared not to have a full understanding of the PSNWR's position at closure but perhaps it was not too surprising that he did not want to draw attention to the PSNWR's inability to make a profit and to pay its debenture holders.

Analysing the application on 24 June 1907, an unknown civil servant drew attention to its weaknesses, writing: 'This is an application of a very exceptional nature... [It] is made by Mr Stephens, the engineer, and Mr Rigby, of whom we know nothing. As it is proposed to ... impose on that company [the SR] new liabilities ... it would seem that the Shropshire company or the receiver on its behalf should have concurred in the application. The Shropshire company has not done so, but on the other hand they have sent in objections to some of the proposals and have asked for protection in some other respects. We have not heard from the receiver, nor is there anything to show that he has had notice of this application. ... There are no drawings except a 1 in Ordnance map, and there is no information as to the present state of the works and equipment. It is therefore impossible to criticise the estimate.

'The proposal is that the money should be raised by the Shropshire company ... It seems to me that if the Shropshire company can raise the money, the interposition of a new company will only give rise to endless disputes between the two companies. There is no provision that the Shropshire company shall have any control over the expenditure of the money either on the capital or revenue account. To get over this initial difficulty the Shropshire company ask for the power to appoint

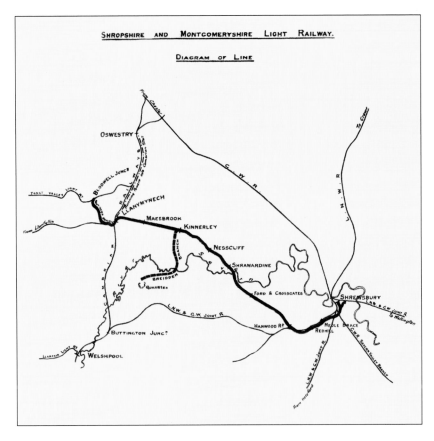

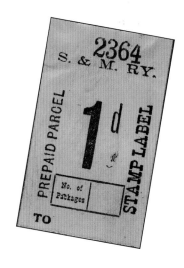

A plan of the SMLR as used by the company before 1921; the running powers to Oswestry are indicated but were never exercised.
National Archives

a certain number of directors. This may mean entire control or no control at all. Already the Shropshire company object to the present provision out of revenue for depreciation and reserve, and there is nothing in the order as to the ownership of the works and equipment paid for out of the money raised by the Shropshire company ...' Of course, as noted on page 51, the SR was not going to raise any money itself.

The possibility of confusion with the North Staffordshire Railway when either railway was referred to by its initials prompted Stephens to write to the BoT on 13 May 1908, asking if the name could be changed to the Shropshire & Montgomeryshire Light Railway. He added that as the Montgomeryshire County Council had taken powers to subscribe to the proposed company, 'the change will appeal to local sentiment'. Stephens probably did not know that the Shropshire & Montgomeryshire Railway Company had been registered at the joint stock companies registry on 1 October 1853. One of that company's promoters had been Henry James Noyes, secretary to the Staines, Wokingham & Woking Railway; an S. F. Noyes had been the solicitor for the PSNWR, SNWR etc. bills – the purpose of the company was 'the construction of a railway from Shrewsbury .... via the valley of the River Rea to Newtown ... and from Caer Flos ... through Welshpool to Oswestry ...'

Although the major companies did not object to the order they did require clauses for their protection and some delay in processing it was caused by the GWR's intransigence over connections with the Hereford and Wellington lines. The objection was protectionist, in so far as it claimed that the Hereford line's junction's existence would prevent the diversion of traffic to the Cambrian at Llanymynech. Stephens, on the other hand, complained that as its cost was an unknown quantity he should have some flexibility over its installation.

The need to get court approval for the clauses and schedules that affected the SR also caused delays, the SR's debenture holders having approved the order as early as 7 January 1908.

Eventually, the order was sealed on 11 February 1909 and was signed by the BoT's president, Winston S. Churchill. Containing 74 clauses and three schedules, it was quite wide-ranging in scope.

The Shropshire & Montgomeryshire Light Railway Co was incorporated and was to have five directors, three elected by the shareholders and two nominated by the SR. The first directors were Stephens, Rigby and the Earl of Bradford.

The railway authorised included the line between Llanymynech and Shrewsbury, the Breidden branch, and junctions with the Wellington and Hereford lines. As defined in the SR's 1888 act, the Wellington line junction was to be opened with the remainder of the railway, but this was not a requirement if the Hereford line junction was made. The Nantmawr branch was excluded from the railways authorised and the Cambrian's rights over it were protected. Except for the Breidden branch, the works were to be started within 12 months of making the order and completed within 18 months. The Breidden branch was to be completed within 18 months of consent for its reconstruction being given by the SR, provided that was within two years of the remainder of the railway being reopened.

As agreed previously, the SR could issue up to £40,000 in 'prior-charge debenture stock' on request of the SMLR providing that half of the SMLR's £2,000 capital had been issued. Holders of the debenture stock were entitled to vote at meetings of both the SR and the SMLR.

The local authorities, Shropshire and Montgomeryshire county councils, Shrewsbury town council and Oswestry, Forden and Atcham rural district councils were permitted to invest in the SMLR, either by making loans secured on debentures or by taking share capital, a sum totalling £5,750.

A legal agreement made between the promoters and the SR to define the relationship between the two companies was incorporated in the order as a schedule. *Inter alia*, it required the SMLR to equip the railway with not less than £5,000 of 'proper engines' and rolling stock. After the payment of working

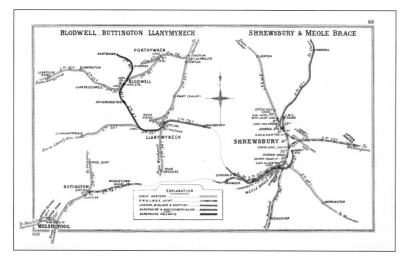

the SR decided to apply for a court order that any monies held in court or by the receiver should be paid to the bondholders.

The first meeting of the SMLR's board took place on 26 February 1909. Bradford, Rigby and Stephens were present, with the first acting as chairman and the last as secretary. After dealing with administrative matters, Bradford resigned as a director and was replaced by W. A. Wardley. The meeting closed with Rigby proposing a vote of thanks to the earl for his assistance in connection with the promotion of the order. A qualifying shareholding (£50) was registered to the directors on 26 March 1909.

One way of resolving any intra-company conflict, as feared by the civil servant in 1907, would be for one company to control the other. In a way this was achieved on 15 July 1909, when the transfer of 254 mortgage debenture bonds, £9,875 first debenture stock, £5,000 second debenture stock and £39,029 11s ordinary stock as well as £963 ordinary stock from Whadcoat to Stephens was registered by the SR. It was noted that the 'secretary called attention ... that the transfers ... comprised the entire holding ... of Mr J. H. Whadcoat'. Stephens was appointed a director in place of Whadcoat. As Stephens had already been elected managing director of the SMLR at a general meeting held on 26 March 1909 he was now effectively in control of both companies.

When the SR board next met, in Stephens' absence, on 22 July 1909, it demonstrated a measure of independence by electing Henderson as chairman and deferring the nomination of directors to the SMLR board until the reconstruction contract had been approved.

The complicated, and potentially expensive, arrangements over the junction(s) with the joint lines proved a sticking point with Stephens despite his grudging acceptance of them. For this and other reasons an application for an amendment light railway order was submitted in May 1909. The order was not referred to at all in the SMLR minutes although it was submitted to and approved by the SR. It was processed by correspondence and there was no public inquiry.

expenses the net revenue was to be directed first to the debenture interest, then to ordinary dividends (a maximum of 5% was specified), and then to reserves and renewals 'a sum not exceeding what may be under the circumstances reasonable'. Any balance was to be transferred to the SR.

While the application was being processed there were several issues that required the SR directors' attention. In January 1908 a writ was served on the Midland Railway Wagon Co, claiming £1,000 damages and an injunction over the misuse of the company's property; judgment was awarded to the company in March 1910, when £750 damages and £50 for privileges was paid to the receiver. On 12 November 1908 the board declared that it could not 'entertain any applications for shooting rights over the line' after the submission of two applications for this purpose to the receiver. Following a meeting between Barcroft and Whadcoat on 4 November 1908,

Above: **Airey's junction diagram, 1928.** *Author's collection*

Left: **From Meole Brace the SMLR ran parallel to the Shrewsbury & Welshpool Railway, jointly operated by the GWR and LMSR at the time this photograph was taken of ex-LNWR 0-6-0 No 8236 with a Kinnerley-bound goods train.** *WEH-LYN collection*

Below: **A Sentinel locomotive on test at Meole Brace in 1925/6.** *J. Hutchings collection*

The SMLR proposed to substitute a new junction at Meole Brace for either or both of those intended to connect with the Wellington or Hereford lines. It also wanted power to pay interest on the debentures out of capital during construction, to increase line speed from 25mph to 30mph and to enhance its trespass provisions.

The GWR and LNWR objected to the junction proposals, claiming that they were in breach of the rules because the SMLR had failed to deposit either plans or a book of reference. The order, made on 19 July 1910, contained three effective clauses. Concerning the junctions, the railway could be opened between Llanymynech and the Shrawardine river

bridge in advance of the rest of the railway being completed while the Meole Brace junction was to connect with both tracks of the Shrewsbury–Welshpool route. Concerning trespass, an offence would be committed provided warning notices were displayed at the nearest station and public road crossing to the location that an alleged trespasser had been found. Stephens was concerned that as the railway had become an unofficial footpath while it had been closed it would be difficult to break people of the habit of using it when services were resumed. Concerning the payment of interest from capital, a maximum of £1,500 could be used for this purpose, rather than the £2,500 requested. The request to increase the line speed was refused.

Earlier, in January 1910, the SMLR issued a prospectus for £14,000 SR prior-charge debenture stock to 'local landowners and others interested'. It claimed that local authorities had already applied for £3,000 of stock. On 13 January Stephens made an application to the BoT for a 12-months extension to the time permitted by the 1909 order because 'we have not yet been able to raise all the necessary capital'; a six-month extension was granted.

Stephens informed the SR board on 21 March that subscriptions for £1,000 ordinary SMLR stock had been received, permitting, in compliance with the LRO, the release of the prior-charge debenture stock.

The draft contract for the 'construction and equipment of the line for £30,000 of prior-charge debenture stock of the Shropshire company' was submitted to the SMLR board on 10 May 1910 and approved. The contractors were Stephens and Francis Claughton Mathews, a solicitor who had acted on SR matters for the Whadcoats since 1893. It was on 10 May that the SMLR's £1,000 share capital became fully subscribed, for following acceptance of the contract Stephens was allocated 43

ordinary shares and Mathews 40, suggesting that Stephens had been extremely careful with his choice of words when the SR board had met on 21 March.

The contract was sealed on 22 August 1910 when the receiver gave the SMLR formal permission to take possession of the railway. Stephens' formal declaration that he was involved in the contract was made to the SMLR board on 15 November. Most likely the work was carried out by direct labour under Stephens' direction.

The SR's cash held by the receiver and the court were released by an order made on 29 June 1910. After reserving £1,500 for costs the remainder was distributed to debenture holders who were entitled to interest up to the date the receiver was appointed, 11 November 1891, and the debenture bondholders. When the costs of the order had been assessed and paid out of the £1,500, the balance of that sum was to be paid to the bondholders.

The BoT had clearly been unimpressed when Stephens requested a further extension of time on 21 July 1910, writing: 'although ready to commence work we are unable to obtain sleepers'. In giving approval for a further six months the file was annotated: 'the reason given … is hardly convincing'.

Administrative progress was made when the SMLR board met on 1 September 1910. Stephens reported that the SR had given him authority to allocate stock, something that was not recorded in the SR's comprehensive minutes. Nevertheless, the board resolved to allocate £5,380 prior-charge debentures to those persons listed in the allotment register. Stephens' salary as managing director was set at £100 per annum and as engineer and locomotive superintendent at £200 for five years from the opening of the line.

The reconstruction must have started during the autumn but the date and progress were not recorded. The £7,940 raised by

Right: **Fettling the track, 1910/11. As the track gang lifts PSNWR rails for resleepering, many of the old sleepers just fall away.** *T. R. Perkins collection*

Below: **Hawthorn, Leslie 0-6-2T No 6 *Thisbe* and train at Llanymynech. To the left a sleeper crib has been built to carry at least two water tanks and behind, the PSNWR locomotive shed remains *in situ*.** *Author's collection*

15 November was nowhere near enough to finance a contract estimated at £17,480 so funds had to be found from other sources. Stephens reported that he and Mathews had been asked to guarantee a loan of £4,000 from the Capital & Counties Bank in Shrewsbury on 1 September 1910. The board agreed that the loan should be repaid from the proceeds of the prior-charge debenture stock as soon as the line was opened. Another £1,000 borrowed from the bank was guaranteed by the Earl of Powis in January 1912, an equivalent amount of debenture stock being reserved for him as surety. The Earl of Bradford also guaranteed a bank loan and was the registered holder of £1,000 prior-charge debentures.

Stephens' efforts to encourage support by the local authorities were amply rewarded: Shropshire subscribed £2,000, Montgomeryshire £750, Shrewsbury Corporation and Atcham RDC £500 each, and Oswestry RDC and Forden RDC, £250 each; £4,250 in total, it was £1,500 less than the maximum allowed for by the LRO. The Pyx Granite Company's £1,000 investment, made to secure the reconstruction of the Criggion branch, was to be transferred to the Granhams Moor Quarry Company for half its face value when that company took over the quarries in 1918.

A total of £20,904 had been subscribed by the end of 1913; nearly 100 subscribers were local residents contributing amounts up to £100. Local enterprises that supported the railway included the Buildings Material Supply Stores Ltd £78, Ceiriog Granite Co £50, and Phillips Stores Ltd £10. The company's auditor, Sir William Barclay Peat, invested £1,110 initially but subsequently disposed of £270. Peat was a member of the Barclay banking family and his firm developed to become a part of KPMG, today's international professional services firm.

In local newspaper coverage of the reconstruction the blame for the failure of the PSNWR was laid at the door of 'over-capitalisation and extravagance in management'. Whilst the former is certainly true, there is no evidence of the latter. One such report, from an unknown source, described how 'Gangs of men are now engaged carving a way through the long line of jungle with which the permanent way is now covered'. The same account claimed that the Earl of Powis and Stephens were acting as trustees for the debenture funds, an assertion not supported by the SR's minutes. In an account of a meeting held to promote the revival that was chaired by the earl it was reported that the then mayor of Shrewsbury proposed that he should be a trustee, and the earl accepted.

With work under way, Stephens reported to the SR board on 12 December 1910 that he had inspected the Breidden branch and was convinced that if it was reconstructed it would make enough profit to pay the interest on 4½% prior-charge debentures. The board consented to the reconstruction, approved a draft contract and authorised the creation of £8,000

prior-charge debentures, Stephens not voting on these decisions. Afterwards his offer to pay not more than three guineas for a new seal press was accepted.

Legal agreements were the sole topic of a SMLR meeting held on 10 February 1911. Contracts with the LNWR and the GWR 're Meole Brace junction' and W. H. Smith & Son for bookstall and advertising privileges were sealed and approval was given to seal operating agreements with the LNWR, GWR and Cambrian Railways, and an agreement for the purchase of a locomotive from the LNWR.

This was to be one of only two references to locomotives contained in the minutes during the Stephens era and it was to be 20 years later before an LNWR locomotive was purchased; perhaps the minute-taker meant the London & South

Western Railway (LSWR). Stephens had to cast his net far and wide in his search for locomotives for his railways and the six locomotives with which the railway was equipped in 1911 came from very disparate sources. They ranged in size from the diminutive 2-2-2WT *Gazelle*, which weighed only six tons, to an ex-LSWR 0-6-0 and two chunky 0-6-2Ts supplied new by Hawthorn, Leslie & Company and allegedly designed by Stephens himself. In age, the six machines ranged from 58 years for an ex-St Helens Railway 0-4-2T bought from a colliery, to the new Hawthorn, Leslies. There is perhaps more to the story of these new locomotives than meets the eye, for on 5 March 1912 the manufacturer invested £1,725 in the prior-charge debentures. It may be that the debentures represented a final payment for the locomotives.

Invariably described as an 'inspection locomotive', the tiny *Gazelle* was unlikely to have been used during the reconstruction as claimed elsewhere, but it found a home on the Criggion branch after being rebuilt as an 0-4-2T. The back of its cab was also fitted with a small enclosure that was sometimes occupied by passengers, a facility that did not always meet with approval; R. Brock, the vicar of Criggion, complained to the BoT about it on 23 November 1912.

All the SMLR's hauled stock was second-hand. Passenger stock initially was four ex-Midland Railway bogie carriages followed shortly afterwards by six former LSWR four-wheeled carriages obtained from the Plymouth, Devonport & South Western Junction Railway. These were classified in the returns as five composites and five of 'uniform' class. There were two ex-Midland Railway passenger brake vans, too. Goods stock consisted of 16 eight-ton open wagons, ten covered wagons, four cattle trucks, three timber trucks and a brake van. Service stock comprised a travelling crane plus two match trucks, for loading/unloading heavy items at stations without a fixed crane, not a breakdown crane as often claimed, and a stores van.

Colonel E. Druitt inspected the line and submitted his report on 7 April 1911. Describing the line, he said the steepest gradient was 1 in 47, approaching the Abbey station; the sharpest curve, at Llanymynech, had a radius of 10 chains; the country through which the railway ran was generally flat; embankments and cuttings were 'of moderate dimensions', the greatest being about

35ft in each case. The original 24ft-long wrought-iron rails were 70lb per yard. All the sleepers were new; in some places at stations half-round sleepers were used, 'as the full supply of rectangular ones could not be obtained' – unless Druitt was repeating an excuse that he had been given the BOT had been unnecessarily sceptical of Stephens' excuse for a time extension.

There were stations at Shrewsbury, Redhill, Hanwood, Ford & Cross Gates, Shrawardine, Nesscliffe, Kinnerley, Maesbrook and Llanymynech with a halt at Meole Brace. Ford & Cross Gates and Kinnerley were passing places. The terminals and the passing places each had two platforms. All stations had name boards and telephones but only Shrewsbury had conveniences, for both sexes.

Shrewsbury had an eight-lever ground frame with two levers spare. Ford & Cross Gates had a seven-lever frame, with one spare lever, interlocked with a two-lever frame at the western end. Kinnerley had a 13-lever frame with one spare lever; at its western end a single lever worked a siding facing up trains. At Llanymynech there was a five-lever frame and, at the eastern end, two sidings facing down trains worked by separate single levers. All the other stations, and Meole Brace, had a siding worked by a single lever. Except at Shrewsbury, all points and frames were locked by the train staff, a key on the staff or an Annett's key. Meole Brace was a staff section for following trains with a two-lever groundframe on the platform working a home signal in each direction.

There were 25 underbridges, four with segmental brick arches on masonry abutments and 21 with wrought-iron plate girders with masonry or brick piers and abutments. One bridge had seven spans, two had four and one two. The widest span was about 48ft and seven of the largest spans were bridged by girders, cross-girders and rail bearers. All the wrought iron used on the bridges was in very good condition, as were their piers and abutments.

The viaduct across the Severn was 320ft long and 35ft above the average water level. It had six spans, two of 60ft, two of 43ft and two of 40ft; it consisted of wrought-iron plate girders with wrought-iron cross girders 6ft apart. The 60ft spans were carried on piers formed of cast-iron cylinders filled with concrete. The weight of the girders was carried on the concrete; some of the cylinders had cracked and had wrought-iron strengthening bands placed around them. The cracks appeared to be old, opined Druitt, probably due to the expansion of the concrete, and he thought additional strengthening bands would be

Testing the Shrawardine river bridge with the construction loco. It is probably one of the Perkins brothers standing on the river bank. *WEH-LYN collection*

desirable. There was no sign of settlement of any of these piers which were 5ft in diameter for a distance of 10ft above the ordinary water level and 4ft diameter above that.

Deflection tests were carried out with the SMLR's heaviest loco, an 0-6-0T weighing 30 tons and 26ft long. The railway also had an 0-6-0 that weighed 46 tons 11 cwt and which was 41ft 5in long, but these figures included the tender. Two of the bridges gave Druitt cause for concern. Identified only as Nos 8 and 13, he said that they had spans of 20ft 3in and 22ft 7in and girders of an open trough section. They were the only bridges that had not had their timber decks renewed – he thought that the timber should be lifted in order to examine the troughs, although he recognised that this would be difficult because the longitudinal rail bearers, hence the track, would have to be removed too. One of the bearers of bridge No 13 had moved ¼in under load and possibly was not properly seated on its abutment.

There were 12 overbridges, nine on public roads, the rest on occupation roads. Four had brick abutments, cast-iron girders and jack arches. Six had masonry abutments and segmental brick arches. One, a cattle crossing, had rolled wrought-iron joists and timber decking. There was one timber footbridge. All were in good condition.

The line was to be worked on train staff and ticket combined with the absolute block telephone; signals normally passed by block instruments were passed by telephone.

A temporary speed limit of 10mph was placed on the viaduct until check rails had been installed and on bridge No 13 until its loose girder had been secured. At some of the bridges, Nos 39, 40 and 44 were instanced, sleepers required securing to the longitudinal timbers. At Shrewsbury a frame was to be erected around the ground frame to prevent its users from falling down the embankment behind it while working it.

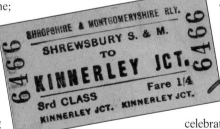

With these relatively minor requirements, Druitt approved the use of the SMLR for passenger use. In the circumstances this report was quite a good result, certainly an improvement on France's effort in 1866. It is unfortunate that there is no sign of the contract to inform us of just what work was carried out.

Whilst the work undertaken by Chambers in 1895 must have made things easier, some of it would have needed revisiting if the complaints made about it by the local authorities were anything to go by. A newspaper report stated that surplus materials from double-track structures were taken down for re-use elsewhere on the railway.

The SMLR's official opening was performed by the mayor of Shrewsbury, Major Charles R. B. Wingfield, on Maundy Thursday, 13 April 1911. Some 200 members of the locality's great and good were invited to travel on the first train to Llanymynech. The mayor climbed on to the roof of a carriage at the Abbey station and toasted the railway from the town's ceremonial loving cup. The special train stopped at Ford & Cross Gates station for a group photograph and again at Kinnerley, 'the engineering headquarters', for an inspection of the 'engine sheds, fitting shops and stores' before proceeding to Llanymynech where they arrived to the sound of detonators being exploded by the train.

There, the guests had 30 minutes for sandwiches supplied by Shrewsbury's deputy mayor, Benjamin Blower. The loving cup had travelled on the train and was passed amongst the guests.

Amongst these was Richard Reeves, aged 82, the guard on the PSNWR's last train and wearing his old uniform. He had been employed by the receiver as caretaker of the line and in 1894 had carried out repairs to railway property at Wern Las and Kinnerley. Kemble, the parish council chairman, welcomed the revival of the railway but complained that there had been insufficient notice to arrange a proper celebration. One report noted that the junction at Meole Brace was under construction, while another said that because of its absence the Cambrian at Llanymynech had benefited from the transport of materials for the reconstruction.

A report in *The Locomotive*, 15 May 1911, commented that the rail chairs were dated 1865 and that 36,000 new sleepers had been laid. The signals at Llanymynech, Kinnerley, Ford & Cross Gates and Shrewsbury had been supplied by Tyer & Co. Intermediate stations were equipped with diamond-shaped stop signals for use by passengers – the lack of comment on this

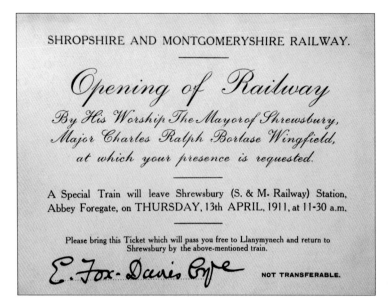

Above: **F. E. Fox-Davies's invitation to the SMLR's opening on 13 April 1911.** *WEH-LYN collection*

Right: **The first train prepares to leave Shrewsbury with ex-LSWR 0-6-0 No 3 *Hesperus* in charge, on 13 April 1911. There is a large tripod-mounted camera to the right of the loco. A cine film was made of the occasion, too.** *WEH-LYN collection*

Below: **Guests descend from the first train on arrival at Llanymynech. Wearing caps and facing the camera at bottom right are T. R. Perkins (left) and F. E. Fox-Davies.** *Border Counties Advertiser*

feature suggests that they were not present when Druitt made his inspection.

The initial timetable had three return workings each day described as mixed, which could be worked with a single train, with running times ranged from 56 to 76 minutes. As the first train did not arrive at Shrewsbury until 9.39am there was obviously no intention of encouraging commuting, while a Saturday evening excursion to Shrewsbury allowed only 25 minutes in the county town. On Sundays, when there were two return workings, trains did not start until after morning church services had been concluded. The options seemed to have been to provide either four hours in Llanymynech or 6 hours 25 minutes in Shrewsbury, or a mere ten minutes there if returning on the first train back.

Above: **The guard has his head out of the window as one of the ex-LSWR 0-6-0s approaches Kinnerley with a passenger train.** *A. M. Davies collection*

Below: **Pictured at Shrewsbury is ex-LNWR 0-6-0 No 8108 ready for a tender-first run to Llanymynech, revealing that the tender still retains its LNWR numberplate. Behind the train a motor lorry is parked across the tracks.** *Author's collection*

Right: **Two days after the opening a train derailed near Red Hill. The photograph was taken during the recovery, where it looks as though the loco, No 3 *Hesperus*, has been re-railed and moved out of the way while attention is given to the carriages. No explanation was offered for the incident.** *WEH-LYN collection*

The public opening took place on Good Friday, 14 April. By 1.30pm a large crowd had gathered at Abbey station and formed a long queue at the booking office to travel on the first train at 1.45pm. Some 250 people travelled, it was reported, with the most popular destinations being Red Hill and Llanymynech.

As much as the directors might have wished the railway to settle into a steady routine that was not to be, for on Saturday 15 April the loco, but not the tender, and three of the five carriages that formed the 6pm departure from Llanymynech derailed near Red Hill. The locomotive was 0-6-0 No 3 *Hesperus*, running tender first. With assistance from an LNWR breakdown gang the line was cleared in less than 24 hours. On the holiday Monday, 500 passengers were carried.

An investment holding company called the Severn Syndicate Ltd, which shared its address with Mathews' office, acquired control of the SR from 28 April 1911. Four substantial holdings, including Stephens' and possibly that of the late W. E. Whadcoat, were transferred, totalling 538 mortgage bonds, £26,775 first debenture stock, £9,600 1891 debenture stock and £97,590 ordinary stock. A further £1,000 of first debenture stock was transferred to the syndicate on 5 December 1912.

The syndicate's function was to supply Mathews and Stephens with the funds needed, in addition to those raised by subscription, for the railway's reconstruction. Identifying the parties to the syndicate can only be speculation although it is reasonable to assume that Mathews and Stephens were a part of it. It is not known if anyone else was involved or why they chose to conceal their financial links to the SR and the SMLR. Neither is it known if the 'syndicate' was just a shell for Stephens' and Mathews' own money, or if money was obtained from a third party or parties. On 28 April 1911 the syndicate was recorded as holding £26,775 of SR prior-charge debentures, and it had a further £1,500 by 30 June 1913. At 4½%, the syndicate would have received £1,272 per annum

from the SMLR; perhaps that was the reason for the anonymity. Stephens and Mathews made themselves personally liable to pay the interest due to the syndicate.

Work on reconstructing the Breidden branch was reported to be in progress when the main line was reopened although the contract was not sealed until 28 November 1911. On 31 December 1911 the SMLR agreed with the Pyx Granite Company, new lessees at Criggion, that the branch would be rebuilt in return for the quarry company committing to transport its stone by rail and to subscribing £1,000 of SR prior-charge debenture stock. Goods traffic on the branch commenced from 21 February 1912. A local newspaper reported that a further £1,500 was required to bring the line up to passenger standards and local residents were expected to make up the shortfall. Whether it was really fit, even for goods traffic, must be open to question for when Druitt made his inspection on 22 May he found serious deficiencies and it was certainly not fit for passenger services. Shades of Rich's experience in 1870. Druitt reported on his second inspection, recommending that the branch be approved for use by passenger trains, on 20 June 1912.

He found that his requirements had been met with the exception of the ballast that required breaking up, another repeat from Rich's 1870 inspection. Like the rest of the line, the branch was to be worked by train staff and ticket and absolute block telephone, Criggion station having been provided with a telephone, trap points and a down home and starting signal to accommodate this.

The river bridge between Melverley and Crew Green was described in detail. There were eight spans, three of which, between 12ft and 15ft 10in, consisted of timber baulks supported on timber piles or trestles. One span, 14ft 4in, consisted of a wrought-iron plate girder under each rail. The other four spans varied between 27ft 10in and 40ft 2in and consisted of wrought-iron girders with cross girders 6ft apart and timber longitudinals. These spans were supported on timber piers composed of piles, the piers carrying the bridge across the river comprising eight piles each driven about 30ft into the river bed and braced together.

He explained that they had shown no sign of sinking and had ample holding power for the weight supported on them. The girders had sufficient theoretical strength for engines and rolling stock not exceeding 10 tons. He tested the bridge with two engines coupled together and found the deflections not excessive. No guard or check rails had been provided and until they were, the speed over the bridge was limited to 10mph. Descriptions of the line in dereliction said the old bridge was very dilapidated and possibly not safe even to walk across, probably evidence of France being short of funds when it was built; once again history was repeating itself.

Stephens transferred some of his SMLR ordinary stock to four of his Tonbridge employees on 5 January 1912. Alfred Willard, Albert Osborne and William Henry Austen had ten shares each and George Willard eight. Stephens retained ten shares for himself.

By February 1912 a number of management positions had been filled. J. L. White, previously an LNWR district inspector at Shrewsbury, was passenger and goods superintendent. John Stockdill, previously in charge of the goods rates department of the London & South Western Railway, was now responsible for rates and fares. A. J. Matthew, previously in the South Eastern & Chatham Railway's accounts department, was audit accountant, and S. J. W. Knott had been appointed accountant.

After the opening there were a number of changes to the SMLR board, some of them very short-lived. W. A. Wardley resigned from 27 February 1912, being replaced by Alfred Malby, recently retired as the London & South Western Railway's chief goods manager. Malby had resigned before the next board meeting, on 30 July 1912, and was replaced by Lewis Daniel Price. The latter submitted his resignation on 10 November and was replaced by Ronald Elphinstone Hall. Hall resigned by 22 June 1915, to be replaced by Arthur Purdy Tabraham. Mathews was elected a director of the SR on 5 December 1912.

The SMLR was not so coy about its shooting rights as the SR, on 30 July 1912 registering an agreement to let them to

Colonel H. P. Hall for £4 10s per quarter. In another attempt to add to the railway's revenue-earning activities the board was to agree, on 19 November 1913, to submit an application to the Postmaster General to become a party to the 1891 'single post letter by railway' agreement whereby the railway could carry letters on payment of a fee. The railway produced its own stamps for the service.

A series of linked property transactions was conducted in 1912/3 that appeared to be 'revenue neutral'. On 19 December 1912 the SMLR sealed a contract for the rental of four cottages at Kinnerley from the SR for £30 per annum, then on 26 June 1913, the SMLR agreed to rent them to the Severn Syndicate, also for £30 per annum. Possibly Stephens and Mathews wanted holiday homes or, more likely, had entered the 'rent-to-let' market.

At a general meeting on 30 July 1912 a 5% dividend was declared on ordinary shares covering the period from the opening until 31 December 1911. At 5%, £50 on £1,000 issued capital, the SMLR was able, apart from the four war years, to pay a dividend until 1929. The shares became fully paid up by 20 April 1914.

After seven years as managing director, Stephens' position with the company was given board attention on 9 February 1916. As he had not accepted the salary voted to him as managing director and engineer in 1910 it was resolved to appoint him as manager at £200 per annum from 4 January 1916 'pending current crisis'. A year later he was awarded a further £25. Because of the war it was necessary to submit these proposals for approval, resulting in a settlement in January 1918 whereby he was awarded £200 for 1914 followed by a £25 annual increase, rising to £300 from 1918.

An injury to a porter guard, 18-year-old Ernest Fardoe, which occurred on 8 July 1913, was properly reported. Fardoe had been using a coupling pole to attach a wagon to a moving loco when he slipped and caught his left hand between the buffers causing a slight injury. Although the incident was attributed to Fardoe's inexperience the railway was instructed to issue instructions that coupling poles were not to be used until the buffers had touched. Fardoe remained with the railway until at least the 1950s, when he was a station agent, and probably retired when it closed.

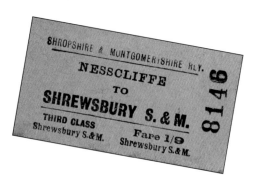

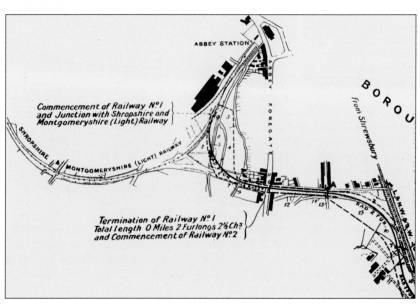

An extract from the plan deposited in connection with the Shropshire Railways (Light Railway) Order showing the proposed layout at Shrewsbury. *National Archives*

A Hudswell, Clarke 0-6-0ST *Walton Park* was transferred to the railway from the Weston, Clevedon & Portishead Railway for a brief period in 1913 but it was moved on to the East Kent Railway within a few weeks. On 19 November 1913, six wagons were hire-purchased from the Wagon Finance Corporation on payment of £147 10s 6d over three years with an option to purchase. As this acquisition was not reflected in the returns perhaps six old wagons were withdrawn or sold, or perhaps the new ones were overlooked. The LSWR agreed to the hire purchase of a locomotive to the SMLR in August 1916; the cost was £701, also payable over three years.

The construction contract was not finalised until 4 August 1916, when Stephens, as engineer, certified that the work had been completed. A summary of the construction accounts included in the minutes show that the Earl of Powis and the Earl of Bradford had loaned £1,000 each, an R. Sandford £100, and T. Ward Green £50. Stephens and Mathews had therefore been paid £23,054 in cash on the £38,000 contract, leaving a balance of £14,946 outstanding. The board agreed that the SR prior-charge debentures be issued to Stephens and Mathews for this amount subject to them not attracting interest until the net revenue of the company was sufficient to pay it. On 22 September, Mathews objected to the open-ended nature of this commitment and on 17 November it was limited to two years. The joint holding was split in 1919, with Stephens taking two-thirds and Mathews the remainder. The reader may wish to speculate whether the SMLR had the benefit of £23,054 or £38,000 of work. No details were recorded about any arrangements for repaying the loans although interest was paid on them.

Stephens and Mathews received another payout from the SMLR in May 1918, when they accepted £956 16s 11d in settlement of any claims against the company for the non-compliance with the contract by the company. The amount consisted of: wages, materials, coal etc. supplied between 1911 and 1914,

Ex-LSWR 0-6-0 No 3 *Hesperus* at Shrewsbury on 19 May 1911.
T. R. Perkins collection

£895 4s 9d; the engine acquired from the LSWR in November 1914 £550; legal charges in June 1915 £39 8s 8d, a sub total of £1,484 13s 5d. The company had already made payments for wages, materials and cash advances totalling £527 16s 6d. Quite why Stephens and Mathews had been subsidising the SMLR after it had opened, if that is what happened, is not clear. It may be relevant that the loans increased from £500 in 1914 to £2,660 in 1915. On 14 April 1920, Stephens reported that '£310 had been credited to the contractors for the loss incurred by delay in payment of the balance on the Criggion branch'.

From the moment the SMLR light railway order application was made it must have been clear to Stephens that the established railway companies would give nothing to the SMLR that they did not have to, and that they would do everything possible to contain it. The order gave it running powers to Oswestry subject to the Cambrian's agreement. The Cambrian did not agree so the SMLR went to the High Court for a ruling, with a judgment in the Cambrian's favour being made on 24 January 1913.

Similarly, Stephens must have had his eye on the Nantmawr traffic right from the start, knowing that it would transform the SMLR as a business. The Cambrian's 99-year Nantmawr branch lease was no deterrent to him trying to find a way in. On 5 December 1912, the SR had given the Cambrian six months notice, as required, that it intended to resume running over the branch with the intention that it would delegate its powers to the SMLR. Nothing came of this move and on 30 December 1916 the Cambrian made a new agreement with the Lilleshall company which was to be used as a weapon to prevent the SMLR from getting the Nantmawr traffic when Stephens tried again after the war. The three railway companies made a new agreement regarding rates in 1917.

One of the three ex-LSWR 0-6-0s owned by the SMLR shunting goods stock at Kinnerley. *WEH-LYN collection*

In common with most other railway companies, the SMLR was taken under government control from 5 August 1914, a situation that appeared to have little effect on the day-to-day operation of the railway apart from the maintenance being even less than usual; only the financial returns were reported while hostilities continued. During the war wages were increased by decree, bringing them in line with those paid by the main line companies. Similarly, fares were increased by 50% from 1 January 1917. This was designed to restrict unnecessary travel and to enable the main line companies to send locomotives and rolling stock overseas, but the policy had the effect of encouraging railway users to seek alternative forms of transport, to the railways' detriment. The first post-war report, made for 1919, reveals that 2,280 prisoners of war had been carried during the year, an average of six per day on a six-day week basis. Financially, the government guaranteed net profits to 1913 levels; independent control was returned on 15 August 1921.

An accident with potentially fatal consequences occurred on 29 July 1915, when the 2.30pm ex-Shrewsbury, hauled by Hawthorn, Leslie 0-6-2T No 6 *Thisbe* derailed on Shrawardine bridge. The train consisted of two passenger carriages, a milk van and a guard's van. The 20 passengers managed to escape without injury. The locomotive is said to have broken a pony truck spring but a photograph (see page 18) shows one of the longitudinal timber beams that carried the track was broken in a manner that suggests, to the author at least, that it might not have been as sound as it should have been. Despite an illustrated report appearing in a local newspaper the incident was not brought to the attention of the BoT. This accident surely explains the early disposal of the 1911-built Hawthorn, Leslie locomotives in 1916, as they will have had a heavier axle loading than the tender locomotives.

The Hawthorn, Leslies were replaced by two more ex-LSWR 0-6-0s that took the same numbers and names; a 1916 purchase has already been mentioned. There is a conflict here with recorded data, in so far as the first 0-6-0 is supposed to have been obtained earlier, when it was the subject of a hire-purchase agreement between the LSWR and the Kent & East Sussex Light

Railway which sanctioned its use on the SMLR dated 19 November 1914. Capital expenditure and receipts reported in the returns do not correlate to these acquisitions and disposals.

Stephens, meanwhile, was involved with military affairs as an officer of volunteer companies in Kent. On 2 September 1913 he was promoted to the rank of major in the Kent (Fortress) Engineers, Royal Engineers, and on 29 April 1915 he received a temporary promotion to the rank of lieutenant colonel. Although he reverted to the rank of major on 4 January 1916 he was for ever afterwards, at least in railway circles, known as Colonel Stephens; it appears that this rank became substantive in 1921.

Another attempt on the Market Drayton extension was started in November 1918, when the SR applied for the Shropshire (Light) Railways Order. The promoters, Stephens, Charles Myles Mathews and the Severn Syndicate Ltd, wished to incorporate the Shrewsbury & Market Drayton Light Railway and build a railway 22 miles long. Capital would have comprised £10,000 ordinary stock and £220,000 in SR 5% prior-charge debentures. Stephens' estimate for the works was £199,095. The application met with concerted opposition from the Cambrian, GWR and LNWR, particularly objecting to clauses authorising the local authorities to invest, pointing out that as they paid rates it was unfair for the authorities to use the money to invest in a competitor. It is a wonder that they had not used the same argument against the SMLR in 1909. After a six-hour public inquiry held in Shrewsbury on 19 March 1919 the application was rejected. In their annual report the light railway commissioners said that the application made the case for better facilities 'in the district traversed', but that it failed because the basis of the financial proposals and the route required reconsideration. This information was not passed to Stephens in the letter informing him of the rejection.

Although the main line railway companies had defeated the Market Drayton proposal Stephens was still not deterred from doing battle over the Nantmawr traffic. He resumed his campaign in 1920 when a light railway transfer order to allow the Cambrian to take over the TVLR was being processed. He asked the Cambrian for running powers to Nantmawr, a mixed train between Blodwell Junction and Llanymynech and a through carriage from Llanymynech, originating at Oswestry, to Shrewsbury.

He succeeded with none of these requests, but must have thought that he was making progress on 27 November 1920, when he persuaded Lilleshall to commit to a six-day trial despatch via the SMLR. This never happened either, because none of the other companies wanted it to happen. The Cambrian's Lilleshall agreement required the railway companies that were not party to it to approve any traffic, so Stephens was just given the run-around. When the LNWR agreed to accept the traffic at Meole Brace the GWR would not. The Cambrian required the wagons to be weighed before they could be accepted, but the Nantmawr weighbridge had been condemned. Lilleshall thought the Cambrian was going to replace it, which it would but not if the SMLR was working the traffic. John Williamson, the Cambrian's general manager, had some of his replies to Stephens' letters vetted by the company's solicitor to protect himself. Stephens' frustration comes through in his letters, particularly those to Williamson, and extracts are worthy of quotation:

- 'I want to see you personally... The Nantmawr agreement seems so complicated that one almost wishes it could be declared obsolete and a new agreement entered into on a somewhat different basis. I am sure we shall never have any comfort as it is now.' (10 September 1920)
- 'We do not get very far with our negotiations, it seems to be a question of putting it off, month after month, in the hope of some catastrophe happening, which will render further negotiations useless. No doubt this is good diplomacy, but it is not practical politics.' (9 November 1920)
- 'I find we wrote to you on [four dates], you acknowledged same on the 7 ultimo, stating you would be writing me shortly after a meeting of your directors ... Is there any chance of a board meeting within the next few months on your line? I know the difficulties you labour under, but if you could let me have a reply ...' (17 November 1920)
- 'Hope you have a merry Christmas, and that your conscience will be clear and that the ghost of the starving S&M Company will not haunt your troubled Christmas sleep.' (21 December 1920)

Stephens persevered into 1921 and on 22 April arranged for the SR's receiver, now Ian Macdonald Henderson, to give the Cambrian the requisite six months' notice of intention to use the Nantmawr branch. In August the Cambrian went so far as to set the rates for passing traffic through Llanymynech station, and then declared that it would charge for a minimum of six miles and £300 per annum. The six miles was quickly reduced to four because it exceeded the Cambrian's maximum permitted rate. The correspondence carried on for some time, but Stephens withdrew from it, leaving it to Mathews. The Cambrian file was closed with the railway Grouping in 1923. No GWR equivalent has come to light.

The Grouping could have seen the SMLR, and the rest of Stephens' empire, absorbed into the large regional companies. Stephens, however, fought a strong campaign to prevent this happening and got the minor railways excluded. As a precursor to the 1921 Railways Act the Ministry of Transport had set up a light railways investigation committee with a view to establishing future policy for the development and operation of light railways.

A questionnaire regarding the SMLR, returned in November 1920, includes information not found elsewhere: motor bus competition had been started since fares had been increased (by ministerial decree, by 50% from 1 January 1917); maximum gradient – 1 in 50; minimum radius, running line 10ch, sidings 6ch; maximum axle load 9 tons; maximum booked speed 20mph, maximum authorised speed 25mph, maximum speed safely possible, 45mph (wishful thinking on Stephens' part?); fencing was quick-set hedges with post and wire in any gaps; bonus mileage of two miles was (still) charged for crossing either of the river bridges; stations, other than junctions, seven; halts, eight; intermediate sidings, one; points locked by key on train staff; 5-ton travelling crane available for use at all stations, 50cwt fixed crane at Shrewsbury, road weighbridges at all stations, rail weighbridge at Kinnerley, cattle pens at principal stations; larger stations had capacity for 20–40 wagons, small stations, eight to ten wagons; Kinnerley workshop carried out all repairs except wheel turning, which was done by main line companies; automatic vacuum brake used on passenger trains, hand brake on goods trains; tender locomotives were not

An unusual combination from the south, ex-LSWR 0-6-0 No 5 *Pyramus* with an ex-LBSCR 0-6-0T during the 1920s.
Author's collection

turned; the maximum load hauled by locomotives, 300 tons; acetylene gas lighting and steam heating in carriages; cost of construction – £40,442, rolling stock – £1,720; works and plant – £572.

On the organisation Stephens noted: 'For practical purposes, this line is grouped and has been grouped for many years, with the KESR, the WCP, East Kent Railway, Chichester & Selsey, Rye & Camber etc. A local clerk-in-charge is employed who supervises details locally, all secretarial, accountants, audit department and rate fixing work is farmed out privately, for a small payment per annum'. He also made it clear that he was very unhappy with the 50% fare increase being imposed, in 1917, without consultation.

When full reporting was resumed in 1919 the railway had 'lost' two open and one covered wagon and acquired three more carriages, four-wheelers from the North Staffordshire Railway according to historian Eric Tonks. A passenger brake was, at least nominally, exchanged for a horsebox at the same time. There were changes on the locomotive front in the early 1920s when three ex-London, Brighton & South Coast Railway 'A1' class 0-6-0Ts, known as 'Terriers', were acquired in 1921 (1) and 1923. The Manning, Wardle 0-6-0T was sent on hire to the West Sussex Railway, otherwise known as the Selsey Tramway, in 1924.

Several changes to the company boards occurred during the 1920s. On 22 February 1923, W. Greer Barcroft, who had been

Above: **Although poorly composed, this photograph deserves its place for showing one of the 'Terriers' in action with a goods train. The locomotive does not have a nameplate.** *Author's collection*

Below: ***Hesperus*** **stands at Kinnerley with a short train from Shrewsbury in March 1939.** *R.W. Kidner/Oakwood collection*

Bottom: **A stone wagon is stabled on the right as 0-6-0 No 3 *Hesperus* waits at Kinnerley with a passenger train.** *Author's collection*

involved with the railway since 1888, resigned from the SR to be replaced by Jeremiah MacVeagh. SMLR director A. P. Tabraham had died by 18 March 1925 and was replaced by S. A. Parnwell. MacVeagh became the SR's nominated director on the SMLR board on 21 May 1929, replacing Parnwell; John Pike was to replace MacVeagh on the SMLR after the latter's death in 1932. Also in 1929, William Rigby retired; he was Stephens' associate and SMLR chairman from 1909. James Ramsey of the Caledonian Railway took his place and Stephens became chairman. From 1920 the SMLR board met only once a year, on the same day as the annual meeting the SR board also met infrequently. From 1925, the GWR routed the Nantmawr stone traffic via the Tanat Valley Railway and Oswestry, closing the branch between Blodwell Junction and the Llanfyllin line.

Ullmer, the SR's secretary and sometime director, died on 5 February 1927; he had come to the railway as an associate of the Whadcoat brothers in 1890. He was replaced by F. L. Beard and when the latter died in December 1929, R. E. Boyce became acting secretary.

The company had enough cash spare to invest £2,250 in consols in 1922, an amount that was increased to £3,993 in 1924. Some of this money must have been the £2,443 compensation received from the government during 1923. The consols were used as security for a £1,500 loan in 1924 and were sold at a loss of £220 in 1925.

In what must have been an attempt to reduce costs, and perhaps to increase traffic, a three-car Ford passenger railmotor, with seating capacity for 40 in each car, was acquired from Edmonds of Thetford in 1923. The annual reports show expenditure totalling £1,263 under this heading in 1923/4. In 1923, 9,109 miles were operated, a figure that doubled in 1925. Photographs show that the unit usually ran in a two-car formation.

Six 10-ton open wagons were added to stock in 1928 and six 8-ton wagons were disposed of in 1931; the War Office failed to distinguish between the two types when it conducted its survey in 1940. The arrival of a Wolseley-Siddeley railcar and rail-mounted Ford lorry from the West Sussex Railway in 1928 failed to make an appearance in any of the company's surviving records; the railcar probably never entered service, and the lorry was out of use by the early 1930s.

The Ceiriog Granite Company, lessees of the Criggion quarries from 1925, had obtained a vertical-boiler, four-wheel shunting locomotive from Shrewsbury builder Sentinel in 1927. The SMLR had provided a test facility for some of Sentinel's new locomotives in 1925/6. The Criggion locomotive remained in use until 1959, and with its relatively low weight and speed of 5mph, it had been the only locomotive to work on the Criggion branch for several years. It was scrapped in 1962.

Fresh traffic was on offer when the board met on 2 July 1930. The British Quarrying Company had taken over the Criggion quarries and had obtained a contract to supply stone for the Liverpool–Manchester arterial road. The company had written to say that it required the stone to be routed to the GWR at Llanymynech. The SMLR response was that the choice of routing was its prerogative; it would make more if the traffic was routed via Shrewsbury. The Criggion branch rail was in poor condition and William Henry Austen, Stephens' outdoor assistant, was authorised to purchase 14 tons of second-hand rail from the Southern Railway, to sell the scrap for £3 per ton, and to employ Sunday labour, at overtime rates, to lay it. Installing the 'new' rail was delayed because overtime payments were in arrears and the gangers refused to undertake the Sunday working. The re-laying was completed by early October.

At the same time attempts were made to sell two of the 'derelict' engines. George Cohen offered £70 for 'the Severn' and Thomas W. Ward, £134 for Beyer, Peacock 0-6-0 No 5, both delivered to Shrewsbury. As the GWR and LMSR refused to accept these locomotives on their own wheels and their value as scrap was deemed to be too low, the board decided, on 9 October, that they should be dismantled as the opportunity

Bury, Curtis & Kennedy 0-4-2ST _Hecate_ apparently shunting stock on the Criggion mineral line. The locomotive was renamed _Severn_ in 1916. _WEH-LYN collection_

Above: **One of the ex-LNWR 0-6-0 'coal locomotives' with train at Llanymynech. The carriage next to the locomotive was built for the LSWR royal train in 1848 and was acquired from the Plymouth, Devonport & South Western Junction Railway *c*1926. Approaches were made to the company regarding its preservation in 1940, but nothing came of it. After a period in the military breakdown train it was sent to the Longmoor Military Railway and scrapped there in 1957.** *John Keylock collection*

Below: **Ex-LNWR 0-6-0 No 8182 at Llanymynech.** *WEH-LYN collection*

presented and their components sold for scrap when the market improved. It also decided that No 8 should be equipped with No 7's boiler and overhauled while No 7 and No 8's boiler should be scrapped. The wheels and axles of No 7 were sold to the Kent & East Sussex Railway at £3 per ton in part liquidation of the SMLR's, unspecified, debt to the KESR.

With most of the railway's locomotive fleet out of use approaches were made to the LMSR for ex-LNWR 0-6-0 coal engines. Two were offered, for £420 and £390, in 1930/1 but were deemed unacceptable. In March 1931 No 8132 was offered for £380 standing at Sutton Oak and purchased; it was reported as working on the SMLR satisfactorily in May. No 8236 cost £375 when purchased on 21 June 1932. No 8108 appears to have been purchased in 1930 but the transaction was not recorded; it might have been one of those rejected. None of these purchases were recorded as capital expenditure.

Of the old fleet, Nos 2, 5, 6, 7 and 8 were ordered to be broken for scrap in July 1931. Nos 5 and 7 had been broken up by November, when work was proceeding on Nos 2 and 8. By 17 October 1933, the boilers from Nos 2, 6, 7 and 8 had been sold to G. R. Jackson Ltd, Wednesbury, for £100. Another old loco, the Manning, Wardle 0-6-0T No 4 *Morous*, on hire to the West Sussex Railway since 1924, was sold to that railway for £50 in 1932.

Ramsey, acting as chairman in Stephens' absence through illness, reported on 9 October 1930 that he had visited the Tonbridge office and found that the SMLR was £15,000 in debt, the major creditors being the LMSR, the GWR and the bank. He need not have gone to Tonbridge to find this out, as the information was contained in the annual reports and was not a new phenomenon; taking the so-called temporary loans and the other unpaid bills into account the company had owed at least £10,000 for more than ten years. Even in 1913, the first year for which the full accounts are available, the company did not have enough resources to pay its bills. The major asset on the balance sheet was always undepreciated capital expenditure (made from revenue), a false figure in so far as the assets had been bought earlier, could not be realised and had since deteriorated in value. This lack of allowance for depreciation was a weakness of all railway company accounts as it maintained assets at their original value regardless of their current worth.

The inability of the SMLR to pay its way was undoubtedly aggravated by the SR prior-charge debenture interest, which fluctuated at around £1,000 annually. A sign that the situation was deteriorating had occurred in April 1927 when Stephens had advanced £539 17s 1d to enable a payment to be made to the LMSR on the traffic account. He had subsequently guaranteed a bank loan of £2,500 'to be drawn upon when required'. From 1927, Stephens did not take his salary although in 1930 the reduction was offset by a salary increase to clerical staff recommended by the auditor.

Although Stephens apparently had a lackadaisical attitude towards financial matters it is difficult to understand why his co-directors, experienced professional men, could take no action about the company's dire financial position until he was absent. Liquidating the debt became the main concern, with priority given to paying the overtime and ensuring continuity of supplies. It may be ironic that whilst the main line companies did all they could to hinder the SMLR they did not, apart from the incident cited earlier, pursue it for the moneys owing to them. With Ramsey in the chair the board met more often and the minutes contained considerably more operational information.

When the board had met on 2 July 1930 the directors had 'expressed their deep regret at the continued illness of Colonel Stephens'. A problem arose because he held one of the keys to the company seal and share transfers could not be properly registered without it. On 26 February 1931 he notified the company that he was incapacitated by the loss of use of his right hand. His absence prompted some concern over administrative procedures when he said that he had authorised J. Arthur Iggulden to sign cheques for him. It was also the practice of Stephens' Tonbridge office to hold pre-signed cheques to issue when required. Iggulden's signing authority was withdrawn on 25 March 1931 and arrangements made for all cheques to be transferred to the London office; in future they would be signed by two directors. On 9 January 1931, Austen had been appointed acting traffic and locomotive superintendent and engineer, backdated to 1 January 1931.

Stephens died on 23 October 1931. In paying tribute to him on 4 November, Ramsey said that he was 'a man with a striking personality and a very warm heart and that this was best exemplified in his unbounded hospitality', concluding that 'not only had they lost their principal colleague but a much-valued personal friend'. The company owed his estate £1,125 for arrears of salary and £373 for loans and advances made by him.

The Criggion stone traffic gave the directors cause for optimism. Traffic averaged 50 wagonloads per day, all sent via Shrewsbury and the £4,483 earned from this source in September 1930 was typical. Walking passes issued to the quarrymen permitted them to use Melverley bridge when the local roads were flooded. Sugar beet had become another source of freight traffic since 1927, although it was seasonal and was affected by the weather; some 2,000 tons was carried annually until 1931. The following year, 1932, this traffic was poor, only 1,108 tons being carried because of the weather, but after a two-year respite the trend was down, falling to 525 tons in 1938.

Over the following three years the level of indebtedness was reduced to fluctuate at around £10,000. The company managed to maintain a good relationship with its bank while slowly reducing its borrowings. By 9 July 1931 the board noted 'very few pressing applications for payment now being received'. It did not make such good progress with the £1,100 it owed the Inland Revenue however, paying a mere £40 per month when the Revenue wanted more.

A programme of track improvements was put in place on the main line. The Southern Railway became the SMLR's source of 'serviceable' double-head rail; 17½ tons bought from Chilworth in 1931 cost £3 5s per ton plus £1 2s 8d per ton transported to Meole Brace, while 10 tons came from Paddock Wood in 1932. The Midland Bank(?) was the supplier of around 5,000 Brazilian hardwood sleepers that could be paid for as used; inevitably some were not paid for. In May 1931, 2,000 oak rail chair keys were purchased for £4 15s. Additional permanent way gangers were employed, with the main line then patrolled and maintained by three gangs instead of two.

Passenger numbers continued to decline and an experiment of issuing return tickets for the single fare was tried in August 1931. As there was no report back to the board it probably did not have the desired result. Another source of passenger revenue came to an end on 30 April 1931. Criggion quarry had agreed to pay a flat £1 7s per week for a workmen's train in February 1918, to run as required; the facility had not been used for some time and the quarry gave notice that it would end the payments.

Savings on the stone traffic were expected after Austen tried one of the coal engines on the improved Melverley bridge and reported that there was no undue deflection on the bridge or stress on the track. Regular use was started on 13 July 1931 despite the bridge not being reported as completed until November 1932. Railcar petrol consumption had increased by 25% to 50 gallons per week despite reduced mileage earlier in 1931. The board decided to dispense with the railcars for the summer service in 1932; their driver, S. Nevitt, had resigned on health grounds in April.

The SMLR bought a second-hand motor cycle for £10 in May 1931 at the behest of canvasser, F. Jones; he was required to maintain it and to take out third-party insurance.

Several changes in personnel took place after Stephens' death. Thomas Ward Green was elected director in his stead on 22 February 1932 and Austen's acting position was made substantive. MacVeagh died in Dublin on 17 April 1932 and on 24 May 1932 Austen and Iggulden were appointed SR directors with Austen becoming the SR representative on the SMLR board.

A meeting with Stephens' beneficiaries, Austen, Iggulden, Alfred Willard and G. H. Willard, took place on 29 April 1932. The beneficiaries agreed to accept 50% of the salary due to the estate, subject to review at the end of the year, but if the railway's fortune made a sudden and significant turn for the better they wanted all of it. In the event they got none of it.

Changes in station facilities were sometimes required to keep up with changing traffic trends. The Criggion refreshment room was moved to Nesscliffe to be used as a store in 1931 and the following year a building used as a clubroom at Kinnerley was moved to Shrewsbury for use as a warehouse.

Government restrictions on road-building expenditure in the autumn of 1932 affected the Criggion traffic and caused the directors to seek economies. Several employees were sacked or put on part-time and the locomotive crew's wages were reduced, a process that was kept under review and which continued into 1933. The midday train was cancelled from 3 October 1932 and from 6 February 1933 the 'afternoon double trip … suspended to the public, but that railcars, or a steam train, would be run … according to the requirements of the traffic'.

A saving of £100 per annum was expected from transferring the telephone and tablet apparatus maintenance contract from the North Wales Power Company to the LMSR. Although the railcar service had been ordered to be withdrawn after 30 April 1932, they still ran nearly 8,000 miles during the year, half the

Gazelle **was provided to haul an excursion for the Birmingham Locomotive Club on 30 April 1938.** *John Keylock collection*

mileage of 1931, and in 1933 they ran 5,146 miles. It is not altogether clear why railcar use declined, and it does not seem to be completely because of the reduction in passengers. They had run 36,000 miles in 1928, their best year.

It had been the company's practice to transfer £125 per month to a special account to pay the prior-charge debenture interest. Arising from the reduction in traffic the board ordered the allocation to be suspended from 1 November 1932. This was the first threat to the interest since the railway had opened; the ordinary dividend had not been paid since 1931. It was decided to ask the holders of more than £100 if they would agree to accept a share of the company's net revenue, even if that meant receiving less than the interest they were entitled to.

On 1 March 1933 it was reported that Iggulden and the Willard brothers had given, and then withdrawn, their assents to the scheme. The Severn Syndicate Ltd, of which Iggulden was a director, also dissented; between them they held £14,371 of the debentures. They applied for the interest that had been due on 1 January 1933 and on being informed that no funds were available, the syndicate and the Willard brothers petitioned the Court of Chancery for the appointment of a receiver and manager, recommending Iggulden for the appointment. The directors resolved to resist the petition but agreed that if an appointment was to be made they would recommend Ramsey. The petition was withdrawn the day before a hearing set for 7 February.

The directors met syndicate representatives on 28 March who agreed to assent to the scheme of arrangement. However, later in the year, the syndicate requested the issue of £279 3s in debentures to represent the interest owing. The company responded that in view of the personal guarantee given to the syndicate by Stephens and Mathews the syndicate should pursue the issue with their respective executors. When the interest moratorium expired in 1937 the holders agreed to a five-year extension.

Aspects of the infrastructure, both on and off the railway, were an issue in May 1933. At Llanymynech, Henry Pooley & Son informed the company that the weights and measures inspector had condemned the weighbridge because it was old and obsolete, while at Shrewsbury the corporation had asked for a £50 contribution towards repairs to Rocke Street, where the railway was a frontager. The weighbridge was to be scrapped and the ground made good and the corporation was informed that the railway could not afford the £50 at the present time. On 29 October 1937 a shed at Llanymynech was destroyed by fire, the company receiving a £250 settlement from its insurance company.

The finances were obviously tighter than usual, because in October 1933 the bank threatened to withdraw the £500 overdraft facility on the general revenue account unless it was guaranteed; the directors agreed to act as guarantors. The Earl of Bradford renewed his guarantee of a £1,000 bank loan for five years from June 1935. The directors did not take their fees after 1932.

The following month, passenger traffic had declined so much that the service was suspended from 6 November in the interest of economy. Passengers carried in 1933 were just over

a third of the 9,142 conveyed in 1932. Goods train revenue was only £5,001, compared with £9,772 the year before and train operation made a loss (£816) for the first time. Despite the passenger service being withdrawn, bank holiday specials continued to be run, and over the next five years 1,716 passengers were carried and the coaching stock ran 963 miles. In 1934/5 the railcars ran 4,940 miles before making their swansong of 204 miles in 1936. In the absence of the passenger train the locality was served by a 30cwt Chevrolet bus 'but the accommodation afforded is not very luxurious' it was said. Lacking covered accommodation for them, the carriages were stored in the open at Kinnerley and Shrewsbury.

Sadly, the opening of the Anglo-American Oil Company's oil and spirit depot adjoining the Shrewsbury terminus in June 1934 did little to help the company despite generating 2,538 tons of traffic by the end of the year. By 1937 this figure had reached 5,157 tons.

Another serious incident had occurred on 23 September 1930, when the railcars were derailed one night and considerably damaged. An internal inquiry concluded with the driver being sacked. During the year £75 was spent on railcar repairs, undoubtedly a portion of it due to the accident which, once again, was not reported. In February 1936 another incident was reported in *The Times*. A goods train ran into five horses at Chapel Lane crossing on the Criggion branch. The animals belonged to Harry Davies of Melverley Hall; two were killed outright and a third was put down later.

After several years out of use, and looking increasingly derelict, *Gazelle* was overhauled at Kinnerley in 1936 and returned to service the following year. The tramcar body having rotted beyond repair, the Wolseley-Siddeley railcar body was mounted on the tramcar chassis for *Gazelle* to pull, the ensemble being used for inspections and special parties. The Birmingham Locomotive Club was one such special party, organising probably the first enthusiast tours of the SMLR, on 23 and 30 April 1938.

A link with the past was broken in 1937 when the land formerly occupied by the PSNWR's loop line to Potteries Junction, some nine acres, was sold to Shrewsbury Corporation.

On the outbreak of war in 1939 the SMLR received a letter dated 1 September informing it that under the Defence of the Realm, Defence Regulations 1939, the railway was now under government control. It was the last of 11 in a list of railways affected. The only other light railways were the East Kent Light Railway and the Kent & East Sussex Light Railway, two other lines once run by Stephens, and probably selected because of their strategic significance.

By the end of 1939 the SMLR owed £16,439 offset by less than £2,000 of realisable current assets. The remainder on the so-called credit side of the balance sheet was £9,756 of capital expenditure paid from revenue and £4,929 of accumulated losses. Of the five locomotives owned by the railway, only one, No 2, the former No 8108, was in use; the SMLR was really in a pretty poor state.

LOCOMOTIVES AND ROLLING STOCK

Right: The Manning, Wardle 0-6-0Ts used by France during construction and passed on to the PSNWR were of the same class as *Queen*, seen on the Shut End Collieries & Ironworks Railway. *G. M. Perkins*

Middle: Bradford, originally *Viscount*, was one of France's Manning, Wardles that passed to the PSNWR. Sold in 1888, it lasted in industrial service until scrapped by the National Coal Board in 1960. It was photographed at Manchester Collieries Ltd's Walkden yard on 27 April 1947.
J. Peden/V. J. Bradley collection

Below: Gazelle was the most photographed of all the SMLR locomotives, possibly because it was usually to be found at Kinnerley when the enthusiasts visited. It was built in King's Lynn for a local businessman, William Burkitt, who used it for private trips over the Great Eastern Railway and the Midland & Great Northern Joint Railway. It is claimed that on one occasion *Gazelle* went as far as Chesterfield, a journey that could not have much to commend it for such a small locomotive, either in terms of comfort or timeliness. This well-known photograph contrasts *Gazelle* with a GER 4-4-0. *T. R. Perkins collection*

Above: The scrap metal dealer, T. W. Ward, offered *Gazelle* for sale in 1910 and it was bought by the SMLR in February 1911, being delivered to Kinnerley where it was photographed with 0-6-0ST No 4 *Morous* on 19 May. T. R. Perkins is standing on the locomotive. *T. R. Perkins collection*

Left: Gazelle was allegedly sent to W. G. Bagnall of Stafford twice, first for rebuilding as an 0-4-2 and then for the cab to be partially enclosed, as seen here, but it is more likely that the work was actually carried out at Kinnerley as there is no record of the work being undertaken in the Bagnall archives. As modified, it operated Criggion branch services for several years. *T. R. Perkins collection*

Bottom: In the 1930s *Gazelle* fell out of use and was abandoned in Kinnerley yard; the photograph here might have been taken when it was being assessed for overhaul in 1937. Originally, most of the SMLR locomotives carried cast ownership plates as shown on *Gazelle's* splasher. The carriages had rectangular plates, presumably because it was felt necessary to distinguish SMLR property from that of the SR. *WEH-LYN collection*

Above: **SMLR 0-4-2ST No 2 was acquired by the SMLR in 1911 and named *Hecate*. Built in 1853, it was much altered during its career and before delivery to the SMLR was reconditioned by W. G. Bagnall. By no stretch of the imagination could it be described as attractive.** *Author's collection*

Below: Hecate **was renamed *Severn*, with brass nameplates affixed as shown, in 1916.** *A. M. Davies collection*

Top: In 1937, *Gazelle* was restored to service for use on inspection and directors' trains. In later years Austen's son was to recall to Mike Hart a childhood convalescence in Shropshire, the air being better there than in Tonbridge, and being taken to the SMLR for an excursion with *Gazelle*. *WEH-LYN collection*

Below: After many years confined to the Criggion branch, *Severn*, too, fell out of use and after several years when literally put out to grass it was broken up at Kinnerley. It was photographed partially dismantled on 14 April 1930. The tank on the ground belonged to No 8 *Dido*. One of the SMLR's cattle trucks is stabled in front of the loco. *WEH-LYN collection*

Above: **Acquired in January 1911, 0-6-0 No 3 *Hesperus* was the first of three LSWR 'Ilfracombe goods' locomotives owned by the SMLR. Hauling the inaugural train in 1911 it was, after *Gazelle,* pretty much the railway's 'celebrity' locomotive and its time in traffic exceeded that of its classmates. This photograph was probably taken in 1911.** *F. E. Fox-Davies*

Below: **No 3 later received cast *Hesperus* nameplates, as seen in this 1927 photograph taken at Llanymynech.** *Michael Whitehouse collection*

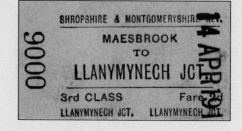

SHROPSHIRE & MONTGOMERYSHIRE R...
MAESBROOK
TO
LLANYMYNECH JCT
3rd CLASS   Fare 2d
LLANYMYNECH JCT.   LLANYMYNECH JCT.
0000
14 APR 19...

Above: **A works photograph of Hawthorn, Leslie 0-6-2T No 5 *Pyramus*.** *WEH-LYN collection*

Left: **The other side of classmate Hawthorn, Leslie 0-6-2T No 6 *Thisbe* was captured when photographed on the SMLR, by which time cast nameplates had been fitted. They had LSWR-style livery and were rarely photographed. They were disposed of *c*1916.** *Author's collection*

Below: **Two more ex-LSWR 0-6-0s were obtained as replacements for the Hawthorn, Leslies although, as noted on page 72, the chronology does not quite fit, the 'new' locomotives being obtained in 1914 whilst the 'old' ones were not disposed of until *c*1916. The second No 5 *Pyramus* is illustrated in plain livery.** *A. M. Davies collection*

Top: **The second No 6 *Thisbe* was photographed on 26 August 1926 with ownership lettering on the tender and a plate on the cab side.**
H. C. Casserley/A. M. Davies collection

Above: **Three ex-LBSCR 0-6-0T 'Terriers' were acquired between 1921 and 1923. They were numbered 7, 8 and 9 and named *Hecate*, *Dido* and *Daphne* respectively. The unknown photographer managed to capture them together, from left, *Daphne*, *Hecate* and *Dido*, all with nameplates and their airpumps which they retained even though they were equipped with vacuum brakes for the SMLR.**
Author's collection

Right: **Possibly when first acquired, *Dido* ran for a time without nameplates.**
A.W. Croughton

Top: **No 7** *Hecate* **in its LBSCR guise as No 81** *Beulah***; that name, a locality in south London, is as distinctive as those of classical origins so much liked by Stephens.** *WEH-LYN collection*

Left: **No 9** *Daphne* **seen in the Eastleigh Works paintshop after withdrawal from the SMLR capital stock in 1931.** *WEH-LYN collection*

Below: **Three ex-LNWR 0-6-0s were obtained in 1930-2, the first of them being No 8108, seen here at Kinnerley locomotive shed in company with an ex-LSWR 0-6-0.** *A. M. Davies collection*

Top: **The second LNWR 0-6-0 to arrive was No 8182 which, exceptionally, had no smokebox numberplate.** *WEH-LYN collection*

Right: **The last of the LNWR locos was No 8236. The LMS lettering may be discerned on the tender side.** *WEH-LYN collection*

Below: **Towards the end of 1937, No 8108 was the beneficiary of some attention at Kinnerley, having its smokebox replaced and being retubed and repainted. Its wheels were also sent to Crewe for turning. In May 1939 it appeared in a green livery and with a new number, 2. During the war the locos were repainted in camouflage livery and reverted to their LMSR numbers.** *Author's collection*

Left: **In 1950, after ownership of the SMLR had been transferred to the BTC, the three ex-LNWR 0-6-0s were sent to Swindon for scrapping; No 8108 was photographed there on 24 September.** *Hugh Ballantyne*

Below: **During the ten years from 1947, 21 WD 'Austerity' 0-6-0STs were transferred to and from the SMLR, represented by this photograph of Nos 188 and 193 at Kinnerley on 18 March 1960.** *Hugh Ballantyne*

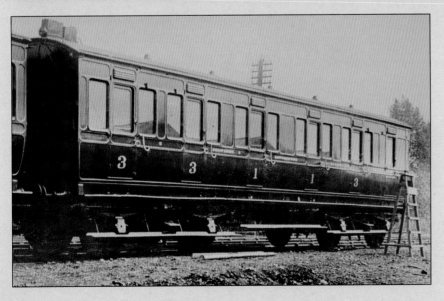

Left: **For passenger stock, the SMLR initially had four ex-Midland Railway bogie carriages; two all-thirds and two brake composites. One of the latter, No 5 in the SMLR fleet, is seen here, probably in 1911. The railway also had two ex-MR four-wheel passenger brake vans, all six vehicles being used on the inaugural train in 1911.** *WEH-LYN collection*

Top: **All subsequent carriage acquisitions were four-wheeled, these being six ex-LSWR carriages obtained from the Plymouth, Devonport & South Western Junction Railway in 1911, and three North Staffordshire Railway carriages acquired *c*1916. The photograph shows two ex-LSWR vehicles, an all-third and a third-brake, in their 'mouldering' stage.**
C. Cairns

Right: **This ex-Great Eastern Railway brake/third was obtained from the Kent & East Sussex Light Railway *c*1919. The three-plank wagon on the far right is lettered S&MR.**
WEH-LYN collection

Bottom: **This exotic vehicle had once, in 1848, been a part of the LSWR royal train. Its acquisition during the 1920s from the Plymouth, Devonport & South Western Junction Railway does not appear to be reflected in the railway's returns. Even when very old and greatly neglected it was said to have been very comfortable.**
L. W. Perkins/A. M. Davies collection

Top: **During its career on the SMLR *Gazelle* had two trailers, the first being No 16, originally a double-deck London horse-drawn tramcar. Probably obtained *c*1916, it was taken out of use with *Gazelle* in the 1930s, and the body rotted beyond repair following a few years of outside storage.**
A. M. Davies collection

Below: **When *Gazelle* was resuscitated in 1937 the tramcar underframe was adapted to carry a modified Wolseley-Siddeley railcar body. The trailer lasted only until 1939, when the body was grounded at Kinnerley, remaining there until 1986.**
A. M. Davies collection

Above: A line of seven out-of-service carriages stabled in the Criggion branch bay platform at Kinnerley in September 1935. *WEH-LYN collection*

Left: Amongst the carriages obtained by the War Office for the SMLR were eight bogie vehicles that had once run on the London, Tilbury & Southend Railway; No 3202 was photographed on 21 September 1958. *R. F. Roberts*

Below: The Ford railcar set at Kinnerley. These vehicles must have been both uncomfortable to drive and to travel in. In the 21st century ear defenders would be a requirement for all. *WEH-LYN collection*

The Wolseley-Siddeley railcar unit 'out to grass' at Kinnerley. In 1937 its body became *Gazelle's* trailer. *Author's collection*

This wagon, the only PNSWR vehicle to survive the cull of stock in 1888, became a part of the SMLR fleet and remained in use, probably as mobile storage, until the 1930s. *F. E. Fox-Davies*

This wagon was seen at Kinnerley in 1958. Its buffers seem to be positioned to enable it to be coupled to *Gazelle,* but there is no record of its use. *A. M. Davies*

The War Office Railway and the SMLR's demise

The war gave the SMLR a new lease of life, but not straight away. Until January 1941 things carried on much as they had done before. The winter of 1939/40 was, however, extremely severe and played a cruel trick on the railway. On 27 January 1940 the Melverley river bridge was damaged by ice, with six piles and their bracings washed away, 'rendering the bridge unsafe for traffic'. Crew Green, Llandrinio Road and Criggion were isolated from the railway as were 64 stone wagons. A report was sent to the Ministry of Transport and the Railway Executive.

It was May 1940 before the company learned the terms by which the government would control the railway. The average net revenue of 1935, 1936 and 1937 was guaranteed; as the SMLR had made a loss it would receive just £1. Maintenance, including renewals, would be allowed on the basis of the average expenditure of those three years, £900. No provision would be made for paying the SR prior-charge debenture interest. Clearly, being under government control was not going to be of much benefit to the railway. The board decided to press for special consideration in respect of arrears of maintenance and the repair of the Melverley bridge.

Ramsey had a meeting with the GWR's general manager, Sir James Milne, representing the railway executive, on 28 May 1940. The following day the board agreed to write to Milne that the main traffic, from Criggion, could be handled via Llanymynech and the section between Kinnerley and Meole Brace could be closed with the track recovered for reuse or sold. The board was prepared to accept this provided the Executive agreed to repair the line between Criggion and Llanymynech, and between Meole Brace and Shrewsbury, and the British Quarrying Company would guarantee a minimum tonnage for a period of years. If the proposals were acceptable, the letter concluded, 'some mutually advantageous arrangement could probably be made for the provision of locomotive power on the two severed portions of the railway'.

Milne replied on 3 June that the proposals were acceptable and that British Quarrying was willing to contribute £500, a third of the estimate, towards the bridge repair and to guarantee 30,000 tons per annum for three years. However, British Quarrying had second thoughts about the guarantee and the matter was left to await developments.

Later in the year, 29 October 1940 is the earliest date in the file, the War Office decided that the SMLR could be used, under military control, to serve a new ammunition depot. The depot was to replace existing facilities at Wem and Nantwich and be capable of accommodating 50,000 tons of ammunition; 50 ammunition sheds would be required, not less than 200 yards apart. A reconnaissance was made on 4/5 November. One of those involved at the WO then was Major Dennis McMullen who, as colonel, was to inspect the Talyllyn and Festiniog railways in the 1950s. The WO team's London bias was betrayed, incidentally, by reference to 'Abbey Road' station.

A War Office plan of developments proposed for the depot at Ford, dated 27 November 1941. *National Archives*

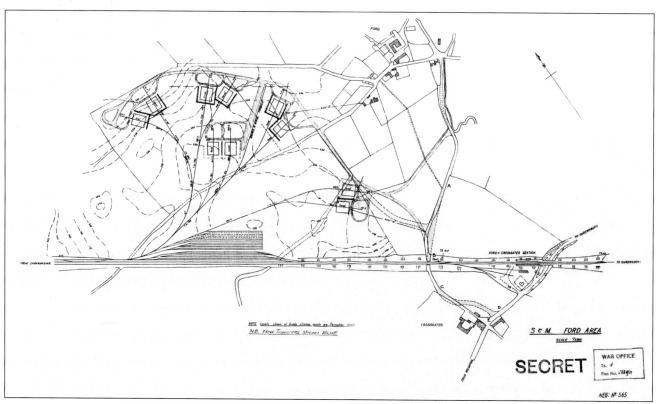

Table 2

Employees subject to transfer to War Department, January 1941

Permanent Way Department

		Date of birth	Date joined company	Wage (weekly)	Residence
Crump, F. G.	Ganger	30 April 1895	28 March 1918	£2 14s	3 Sefton Villas, New Road, Meole Brace
Williams, W. A.	Ganger	19 September 1877	10 October 1910	£2 16s	Shoothill Crossing Cottage, Ford
Mansell, H. W.	Ganger	25 February 1882	January 1916	£2 14s	The Cobs, Wern Las
Frost, E.	Underman	13 June 1909	22 March 1928	£2 8s	3 Drawell, Shrewsbury
Williams, E.	Underman	14 March 1877	11 July 1913	£2 8s	2 New Street, Ford
Lewis, E.	Underman	28 November 1872	1 October 1918	£2 8s	Ash Tree Cottage, Pant
Richards, G.	Underman	30 March 1896	4 September 1939	£2 8s	Holly Tree Cottage, Knockin Heath
Mansell, E.	Underman	21 December 1909	15 April 1931	£2 8s	2 Station Houses, Kinnerley

Locomotive Department

		Date of birth	Date joined company	Wage (weekly)	Residence
King, F.	Driver	20 July 1882	20 September 1912	£4 3s	4 Bungalow, Kinnerley
Mansell, J.	Fireman	28 December 1921	14 December 1938	£2 8s 6d	Wern Las Cottage, Maesbrook

Shop and artisan staff

		Date of birth	Date joined company	Wage (weekly)	Residence
Owen, C.	Fitter	23 September 1880	September 1911	£3 16s	Bankfields, Kinnerley
Beeston, G.	Assistant fitter	22 August 1910	11 March 1926	£2 17s	Greystones, Llanymynech
Jones, A. M.	Carpenter	29 March 1880	2 June 1919	£3 7s	3 Station Houses, Kinnerley

Traffic Department

		Date of birth	Date joined company	Wage (weekly)	Residence
Jones, W.	Guard	8 June 1905	5 October 1929	£2 17s	Lyneside Bungalow, Kinnerley

The reconnaissance established that the line between Kinnerley and Shrawardine would be suitable for an ordnance depot as it was fairly level and not subject to flooding. The locomotives were adjudged to be incapable of heavy work and would need to be replaced by 'engines which have had a recent railway workshop overhaul'. Goods stock was generally in poor condition; the travelling crane required a new jib, the open wagons required new floors and bodies, the cattle wagons were in poor condition and one of two brake vans was under repair. The coaching stock was 'in a very bad state of repair' and while some carriages could be cleaned up for military use they would require new roofing canvas. In the Kinnerley workshop a Cochrane boiler provided steam for a horizontal stationary engine and two Worthington pumps. A 10in screw cutting lathe was in fair order, the 1½in vertical drill was in poor order and inaccurate, an old planing machine was of little use, and the steam hammer was not in order. There was also a grindstone and a 3ft forge with belt-driven bellows. Approximately 25% of the sleepers were in need of replacement.

After the reconnaissance, it was recommended that the War Department should take over the SMLR, except the Criggion branch, and that existing civil traffic be continued. An area between Shrawardine and Nesscliffe was identified for the ammunition depot. It was proposed that military traffic be routed via Shrewsbury (Meole Brace), with Llanymynech used in emergency. The Shrawardine river bridge formed a good target, it was noted, and 'must be considered vulnerable'. As building materials could be arriving within two months the first phase of construction would involve increasing siding capacity at Meole Brace and Red Hill and the lengthening of some loops.

Government officials met Ramsey, Pike and Austen on 15 November 1940 when it was agreed that the WO could enter the property for the purpose of renewing and/or strengthening track and bridges. When the track was sufficiently improved the Ministry of Transport would relinquish control to the WO.

As there was no scope for expansion at Meole Brace the WO proposed developing an exchange facility at Red Hill, Hookagate. When the plans were discussed with the GWR on

9 December 1940 that railway's assistant superintendent said that the situation was not ideal, but that the difficulties were not insurmountable. When he reminded the WO officials that a site at Honeybourne, conveniently adjacent to the GWR in Worcestershire, had been inspected for use as an ammunition transit depot and was still available, he was told that the SMLR scheme would still go ahead.

Discovering that its powers did not permit the operation of a revenue-earning civilian service if the railway was requisitioned, the WO decided that it would be better to take over the railway by agreement with the company. The SMLR would provide all facilities and labour for handling civilian traffic and WO personnel would operate the trains. In exchange for the line being refurbished and for retaining the civilian traffic revenue, the SMLR would not receive a rental. On termination of the agreement the WO undertook to return the SMLR assets in 'as good a condition (ordinary wear and tear excepted) as existed at the time taken over', a full inventory being taken. Pending completion of the formal contract with the WO an indemnity was given to the company on 6 January 1941.

While these hectic negotiations were in process the increased demand for stone for runway building ensured that

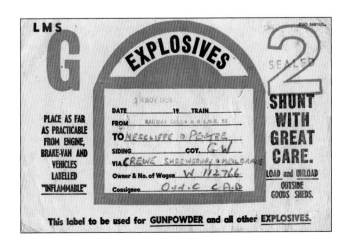

SHREWSBURY ABBEY

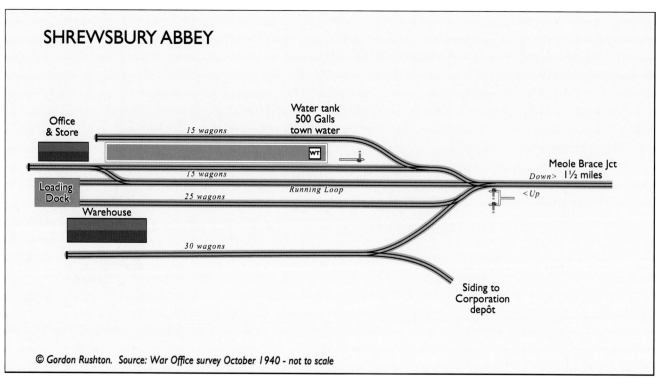

Office & Store

Water tank 500 Galls town water

15 wagons

WT

15 wagons

Meole Brace Jct
Down> 1½ miles

Loading Dock

Running Loop

25 wagons

<Up

Warehouse

30 wagons

Siding to Corporation depôt

© Gordon Rushton. Source: War Office survey October 1940 - not to scale

MEOLE BRACE Jn

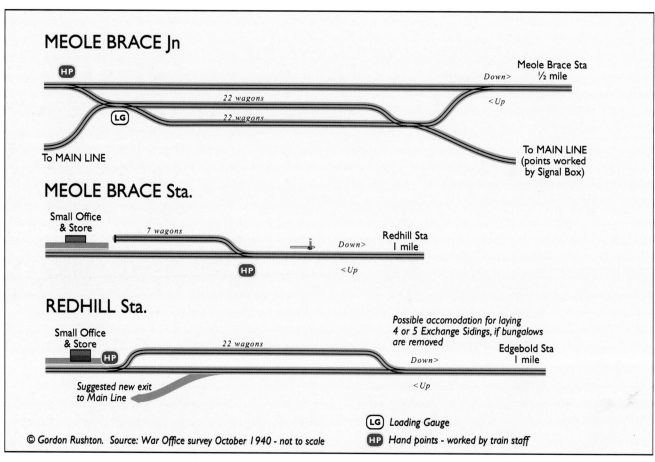

HP

Meole Brace Sta
Down> ½ mile

22 wagons

LG

22 wagons

<Up

To MAIN LINE

To MAIN LINE
(points worked by Signal Box)

MEOLE BRACE Sta.

Small Office & Store

7 wagons

Down>

Redhill Sta
1 mile

HP

<Up

REDHILL Sta.

Small Office & Store

HP

22 wagons

Possible accomodation for laying 4 or 5 Exchange Sidings, if bungalows are removed

Edgebold Sta
1 mile

Down>

Suggested new exit to Main Line

<Up

LG Loading Gauge

© Gordon Rushton. Source: War Office survey October 1940 - not to scale

HP Hand points - worked by train staff

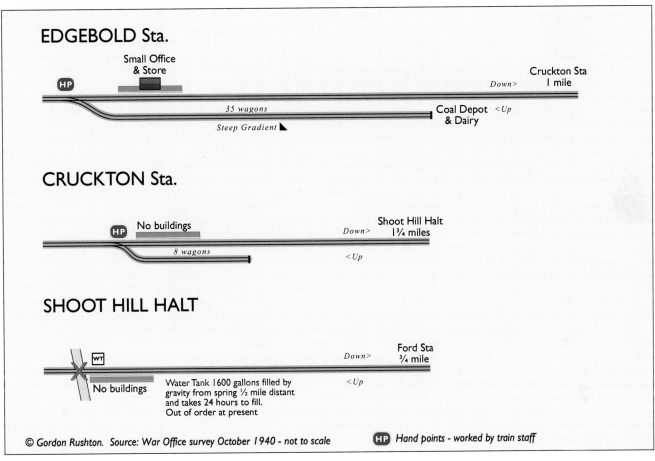

EDGEBOLD Sta.

Small Office & Store

HP

Cruckton Sta
1 mile

Down>

35 wagons

Coal Depot & Dairy *<Up*

Steep Gradient ◢

CRUCKTON Sta.

HP No buildings

Shoot Hill Halt
1¾ miles

Down>

8 wagons

<Up

SHOOT HILL HALT

WT

Ford Sta
¾ mile

Down>

No buildings

Water Tank 1600 gallons filled by gravity from spring ½ mile distant and takes 24 hours to fill.
Out of order at present

<Up

© *Gordon Rushton. Source: War Office survey October 1940 - not to scale*   HP *Hand points - worked by train staff*

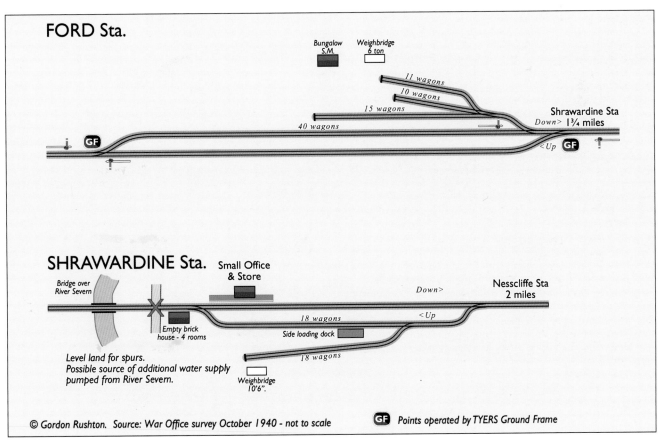

FORD Sta.

Bungalow S.M.

Weighbridge 6 ton

11 wagons

10 wagons

15 wagons

GF

40 wagons

Shrawardine Sta
Down> 1¾ miles

<Up GF

SHRAWARDINE Sta.

Small Office & Store

Bridge over River Severn

Nesscliffe Sta
2 miles

Down>

<Up

Empty brick house - 4 rooms

18 wagons

Side loading dock

18 wagons

Level land for spurs.
Possible source of additional water supply pumped from River Severn.

Weighbridge 10'6".

© *Gordon Rushton. Source: War Office survey October 1940 - not to scale*   GF *Points operated by TYERS Ground Frame*

97

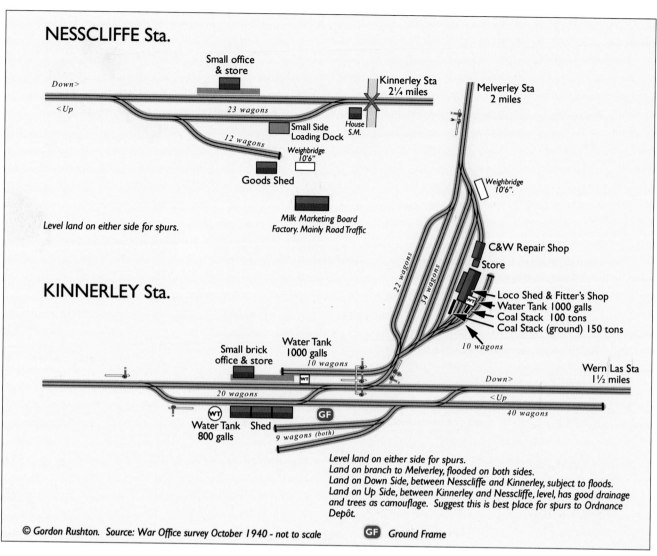

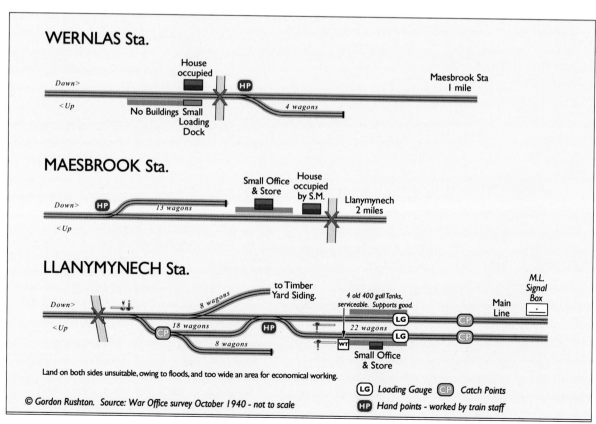

some effort was made to secure the reconstruction of the Melverley bridge. On 8 May the GWR undertook to put the branch and bridge into a condition that would take the LNWR coal engines.

The contractor, Sir Alfred McAlpine, offered two 0-6-0STs at Ellesmere Port and some four-way bottom-emptying wagons to the WO in March 1941, but the correspondence did not note if the offer was accepted or rejected. The SMLR's ex-LNWR locomotives were sent to Crewe one at a time to be made fit for use and by 22 March one had had returned and the second had been sent away.

During a visit Austen saw that uncreosoted sleepers were being used and when he complained, he was informed that it was not policy to use creosoted sleepers on emergency work. Putting his complaint in writing on 9 April 1941 he said that the works were not temporary and that creosote would add little to the cost but add 10 years to the sleepers' use. He was further informed that creosoted sleepers were not available and that as the work was nearly complete it was too late to do anything about it. As part of the WO accommodation work the track between Nesscliffe and just outside Kinnerley was doubled.

A derailment occurred on or about 27 May, but apart from a telegram requesting information no details were placed on file.

The WO, in the guise of No 1 Railway Group, Royal Engineers, formally took over the SMLR main line, and the employees who were not required by the SMLR (Table 2), from 1 June 1941. There was actually no change in the employees' position, for the company continued to pay the wages and was reimbursed by the WO. A similar arrangement applied to the supply of locomotive coal. The employees' families were allowed to retain their privilege of travelling in the goods train's brake van without charge, a facility that took eight letters to confirm (Table 3).

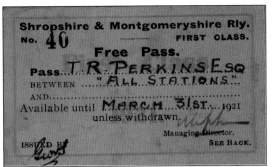

new to the SMLR in 1941; whether the locomotive referred to in the letter was one of those is not known.

The company was informed that the Melverley bridge had been repaired and that the Criggion branch was therefore available for traffic from 27 October 1941. The War Department (WD) agreed to work the traffic for 17s per hour except on Sundays when the charge would be £1 per hour; the rates were increased to 18s 3d and 21s 6d from 1 January 1942. A £2,000 bridge repair fund created in 1931 was closed in 1943 and the provision applied to other purposes.

The WO was the venue for a meeting attended by Ramsey and GWR representatives on 23 December 1941. Ramsey complained that claims for pilferage from the goods train had increased, citing timber, tea and cigarettes as targets and asked for wagons to be brought onto the railway from Meole Brace as quickly as possible. A few months later there were complaints that the railway's own mishandling of goods in transit was the cause of damage and pilfering.

Ramsey also said that he had been surprised to learn that WO engineers had placed a 9-ton axle limit on the Melverley bridge in view of the GWR's undertaking on 8 May. The WO supported Ramsey's understanding of the undertaking, but the GWR denied that it had ever been the intention to strengthen the bridge to carry anything heavier than the quarry's Sentinel locomotive. The arrangement whereby the quarry locomotive propelled the wagons to the Kinnerley side of the bridge for collection continued.

Although the WO concentrated on making the SMLR fit for use, parts of the railway's estate received unwanted attention. Kinnerley locomotive shed was being repaired in January 1941 when a heavy snowstorm demolished a part of it. Repairs, initially hindered by continuing cold weather and the blackout, took some time. When Shrawardine station house was gutted by fire on 1 November 1941, the board noted that 'the question of reconstruction was in hand'; no explanation was offered for the cause of the fire.

At a meeting held between the director of works, the contractor and others on 30 January 1941, Sir Alfred McAlpine, (the man, not the partnership), complained about the constraints of working on a site with no road access and the shortage of locomotive power. He could use eight locomotives yet had to make do with four, but it was pointed out that his staff had only ever asked for four locomotives. The director said that locomotives were difficult to get hold of; he had two small locomotives, one called *Yeovil* [Hudswell, Clarke 0-6-0ST 1529 of 1924] which needed repairs, its wheel flanges were too sharp, and a contractors' locomotive called *Victory* [Neilson 0-4-0ST 420 of 1859] which had broken stays. *Yeovil* was in use by 12 February 1942, by which date there were eleven operational locomotives on the railway, four of them under repair, including two of the new diesels. McAlpine regularly complained about a shortage of locomotives, but his staff seemed happy with what was available.

A memo dated 1 April 1942 reviewed the situation, there now being 13 locomotives on the railway, including one that was hired. Five were out of action: two were being repaired locally, one was to be sent to Stafford, *Yeovil* would have to be sent away, and a diesel locomotive was awaiting spares. Of the working locomotives, four were working for McAlpine, three at Shrawardine and one at Kinnerley. Ford depot was being worked by the train loco. To strengthen the fleet, a new diesel

Table 3

List of passes issued to company's employees July 1941

Station agent	A. Jones and wife
Clerk/canvasser	G. H. Gibbs and wife
Station agent	H. G. Funnell junior and wife
Station agent	H. G. Funnell senior and wife
Station agent	E. N. Fardoe and wife
Porter/agent	W. Davies and wife
Fitter	C. Owen and wife
Driver	F. King and wife
Carpenter	A. M. Jones and wife
Assistant fitter	G. H. Beeston
	(between Kinnerley and Llanymynech)

Mrs W. Jones
(wife of guard Jones) (between Kinnerley and Shrewsbury)

The SMLR locomotive fleet was soon found to be inadequate. Ex-GWR 0-6-0 No 2552, WD No 200, arrived at Kinnerley from the Longmoor Military Railway on 12 December 1941 and, after some minor repairs, entered service on 18 December. On 15 December the WO was informed that 'arrangements had been made to send two additional GWR 0-6-0 tender engines and one additional diesel'. A second ex-GWR 0-6-0, No 2442, had actually arrived on 15 December and entered service the next day. A Drewry and three Barclay 0-4-0DMs were supplied

locomotive was en route from Kilmarnock and No 47, another diesel, was due from Branston within a week; a GWR steam locomotive would be available to be sent to Long Marston when 'the new Hunslet' was run in; two contractors' locomotives had been offered by the Ministry of Works and Buildings which would probably be accepted, even if not entirely suitable. At Shrawardine, 800 tons of materials were being handled per day, but McAlpine needed 1,200 tons a day to maintain the agreed rate of progress.

The Hookagate exchange sidings had been brought into use by 29 January 1942. Already a considerable amount of traffic had been received for both railway and depot construction (Table 4). The first ammunition had been received (346 wagons), and despatched (73 wagons), by the Royal Army Ordnance Corps during the first three weeks of February 1942.

Table 4
Record of loaded wagons received and despatched (for use in War Diary)

January – December 1941

	Railway construction company	Contractors	Public
Received	5,928	5,798	2,389
Despatched	57	54	520

January 1942

Received	465	1,102	203
Despatched	3	3	82

The war and the reconstruction contributed to a considerable increase in civilian traffic in 1941: 122,525 tons compared with 20,984 tons in 1940. In 1942, however, the traffic was to fall back to 49,150 tons.

The original depot at Nesscliffe was followed by others at Kinnerley, Argoed, Maesbrook, Shrawardine, in two parts, and Ford. Eventually there were 206 rail-served depots and a camp station, at Shrawardine. The railway was operated in accordance with the military railways rule book, published in 1938, as modified by local instructions. The lines between Kinnerley and Llanymynech and Hookagate and Shrewsbury were worked with a one-engine-in-steam key. Kinnerley to Nesscliffe east was worked by electric token, the remainder of the line by telephone and ticket. Transfer of traffic to and from the Criggion branch required the Kinnerley–Llanymynech one-engine-in-steam key. Access to sidings at Nesscliffe, Pentre, Shrawardine and Meole Brace was by Annett's key. Block posts were established at Hookagate, east and west, Ford & Crossgates, Quarry, Nesscliffe and Kinnerley. The maximum line speed was 25mph and the axle loading was 16 tons.

In addition to trains run for the contractor, the daily goods and the ammunition workings, the line was approved for the operation of workmen's trains from 1 January 1942 for which 13 'new' carriages were obtained. All bogie vehicles, they came from the London, Tilbury & Southend Railway (8), GWR (4) and LMSR. Four carriages had already been transferred by September 1941, from the Melbourne Military Railway, and 20 LNWR camping coaches were then in use as accommodation at Kinnerley.

The ammunition traffic brought vehicles from far and wide, including four-wheeled vans from French railways, Nord, Paris–Orleans and PLM.

Ramsey died on 5 February 1943, having served 12 years as chairman and managing director since Stephens had died. Pike became chairman and Austen was appointed managing director. The latter's salary was agreed as: managing director £150, fees £50, expenses £125 as well as traffic and locomotive superintendent and engineer £100, as existing, in total £425. On 8 September 1943, Cornelius James Selway CVO, CBE, MInstT took Ramsey's place on the board.

Ex-LNWR 0-6-0 No 8182 at Hookagate with a train from Shrewsbury in June 1947. *Michael Whitehouse collection*

S. & M. Rly.
Military Recreational Travel Permit
No 60179
KINNERLEY
TO
SHREWSBURY
Return Fare 6d.
Permission to travel is granted on travels at his

Table 5

SMLR Tonnages and receipts 1939–1947

	1939	1940	1941	1942	1943	1944	1945	1946	1947
Goods	3,381	11,437	38,730	15,723	14,477	12,966	11,754	10,896	9,532
Coal and coke	1,882	6,853	7,647	6,789	6,211	5,687	5,397	4,953	4,387
Other minerals	16,472	2,694	76,148	26,638	19,764	28,306	26,750	25,887	26,991
Stone traffic									
To Kinnerley (for construction)				12,985	10,210	13,398	179		
Non-SMLR destinations	12,128			1,624	6,261	9,534	22,717	21,304	
Petrol	5,879	4,812	4,069	3,052	1,213	672	259	187	
Sugar beet									
Wagons	58	330	158	181	183	218	226	370	392
Tonnage	468	2,753	1,343	1,434	1499	1,933	1,854	3,384	3,611
Receipts	£4,168	£1,480	£4,307	£10,406	£11,015	£13,410	£20,914	£20,088	
Expenditure	£5,793	£5,953	£5,034	£5,569	£6,112	£6,582	£7,461	£7,298	
Net receipts	-£1,625	-£4,473	-£727	£4,837	£4,903	£6,828	£13,453	£12,790	

No doubt with WO encouragement, a complaint had been made in 1942 about the locomotive shed being cluttered with SMLR 'assets'. These unwanted carriages, wagons and the railcars were sold for scrap in 1943, realising £798.

The operation of the main line by the WO still left the Criggion branch under control of the Ministry of War Transport. The 1940 agreement was reviewed by the Ministry and new conditions imposed, effective from 1 January 1942, but it was November 1943 before the SMLR board considered and accepted them. As a result the SMLR became caught between two branches of government over the interpretation of the agreement with regard to responsibility for maintenance of certain station buildings. On 7 March 1944 the company informed the WO that it was passing the correspondence on to the Ministry in order that the departments could sort it out between them. Some buildings on the main line had not been taken over by the WO, yet if the £900 maintenance budget could only be applied to the Criggion branch the buildings on the main line could not be maintained. Agreement for a more flexible interpretation of the rules allowed the board to record that urgent repairs were being carried out to Ford station yard in March 1945.

The £7,597 4s 5d cost for repairing the Melverley bridge and the Criggion branch had been notified to the board in time for consideration at the 7 March 1944 meeting. A figure of £1,177 would be taken from the unexpended maintenance balance and the Minister of Transport had authorised a special charge be made to the company's net revenue account of the residue. Austen reported that more work was required on the bridge in May 1945.

The company's land at Shrewsbury contained a stone refectory pulpit, formerly part of the adjacent Abbey that had become detached from it when Telford routed the Holyhead road through the Abbey grounds c1820. Scheduled as an ancient monument in 1934, arrangements to transfer control of the structure to Shrewsbury Corporation were completed on 27 September 1944.

With the end of the war in October 1945 the WD asked the company if it could consider taking over the operation and maintenance of the railway and the WD sidings on their behalf, in order to reduce the numbers of WD personnel. The directors agreed to take on the operation, subject to conditions and civilian labour being available; a meeting was to take place at the WO the same day, but nothing more was said of the proposal.

At the board meeting on 27 February 1946 Pike was ill so Selway acted as chairman. Green tendered his resignation and John Pattinson Thomas MIEE, MInstT was appointed in his stead. Austen was awarded a £100pa salary increase. After Pike died on 2 March 1946 Selway was to say that his death was a matter of personal regret: he 'was a man of great conscientiousness and integrity and the company has suffered a heavy loss'. Iggulden was appointed the SR's nominee director of the SMLR on 4 February 1946 and R. G. Davidson FSAA, ACIS, MInstT was appointed a director on 8 May 1946. Iggulden's nomination seems not to have been notified to the SMLR for he was never recorded a director of that company, although he was, however, recorded as attending the last board meeting in 1948.

The Kinnerley station agent, H. G. Funnell, who had been unwell since 28 November 1945, was thought to be unlikely to recover sufficiently to resume his duties. He had been on full pay, £5 3s 6d, until 5 March when he been put on half pay. On 8 May 1946 the board resolved to give him one month's notice to retire and to make him a 'compassionate' gift of £25.

Compulsory trades union membership by company employees was sought by the National Union of Railwaymen, writing on 2 August 1946. The matter was considered on 1 October 1946 when the board noted that a similar application had been made to the main line companies and decided to await developments.

Austen reported, also on 1 October 1946, that the War Department had produced plans for the repair or renewal of nine bridges on the main line, including that over the Severn at Shrawardine and over the Hereford railway line. The river bridge was replaced by a new structure located between the piers of the original of the old in 1947. The old structure was demolished in 1954.

The SMLR was notified by letter dated 28 November 1946 that it was included in the list of companies that would vest in the British Transport Commission on 1 January 1948. The SR was also included in the list of companies to be nationalised. The SMLR board met for the last time on 3 March 1948 when, amongst its normal business, it noted that the company had been absorbed into the Railway Executive, Western Region, and that the transfer of functions was well in hand. It decided that there was no need to call an annual general meeting.

The penultimate item dealt with by the company was the renewal of two bridges on the Criggion branch, at Melverley and near Kinnerley. The Ministry of Supply having decided that Criggion stone was of strategic importance, the Ministry of Transport agreed to make a loan of the £10,512 10s contract price at 2¼% interest to the SMLR for their renewal. The directors had agreed to the arrangement on the basis that the liability for the loan would be transferred to the British Transport Commission on vesting day. The Severn Catchment Board offered £6,000 and the British Quarrying Company offered £1,000 towards the bridges which eventually cost £23,300. The contract with E. A. Farr Ltd of Westbury, Wiltshire, had been signed on 27 November 1947.

On this note the SMLR became a part of the national network although remaining under WO control. The irony was that during the last ten years of the SMLR's independent existence the government benefited by £37,091 from its operation of the railway because of the control agreement. The company lost £3,511 over the same period (Table 5). Of course, the government paid for the refurbishment and new bridges, but the ammunition traffic was calculated to be worth nearly £2 million over six years, so if the SMLR cost the government anything it was not very much (Table 6).

debenture bonds, issued to the Whadcoats in 1890, were valued at 50% of their original capital worth, calculated on the cost of buying out the Nantmawr branch income, which went to the bondholders, over 30 years. The prior-charge debentures were valued at 5% because the SMLR directors argued that with the ammunition depots the SMLR would be much busier post-war and the holders had expectations that it would produce a net revenue in excess of that previously achieved. The BTC pointed out that no interest had been paid since 1931 and thought that the prospect of receiving more was remote.

The first and second SR debentures and the ordinary stock were described as being 'virtually worthless' and awarded a nominal ¼% compensation. The SMLR shares attracted the same valuation, effectively valuing the company at a mere £2 10s. If France had concentrated on getting his stone out of the quarries instead of trying to build an empire, he, and a lot of other people, would have been much better off.

After 82 years and nearly £2 million of capital expenditure, the entire enterprise had a cash value of less than £30,000. The Severn Syndicate was the biggest beneficiary, holding all of the bonds, £28,275 of the first debentures, £9,600 of the second, £6,520 of the prior-charge, and £97,590 of the ordinary stock. Between them, Iggulden, Austen, the Willard brothers and Mathews' executrix had £15,870 of the prior-charge debentures. Austen and Iggulden had small holdings of the ordinary stock.

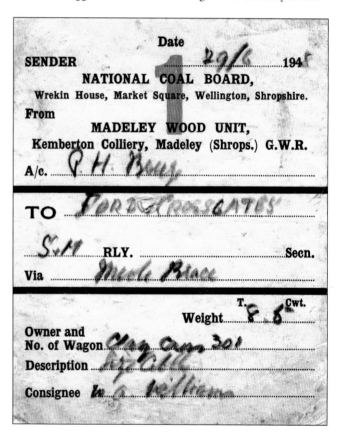

Table 6

War Department tonnage and receipts – 1942–1947

	Forwarded (tons)	Receipts	Received (tons)	Receipts
1942	71,323	£128,380	137,893	£248,206
1943	216,881	£390,385	133,105	£239,588
1944	119,739	£204,739	175,854	£316,536
1945	52,719	£114,694	93,611	£164,498
1946	24,535	£46,456	14,028	£26,652
1947	15,289	£29,059	16,312	£30,993
	500,486	£913,713	570,803	£1,026,473

To complete the nationalisation process the BTC submitted its valuation of the SR and SMLR securities to the Transport Arbitration Tribunal. No one contested the Commission's assertions and the tribunal accepted the assessment. The SR's

Table 7

Shropshire Railways – valuation of securities

Title of old security	Capital amount	Value per £100	Amount of BTC 3% stock at par
5% debenture bonds	£53,800	£50	£26,900
5% first debenture stock	£46,175	5s	£115 8s 9d
5% second debenture stock	£16,600	5s	£41 10s
4½% prior-charge debenture stock	£36,870	£5	£1,843 10s
Ordinary stock	£345,860 13s 1d	5s	£864 13s

The compensation was paid in the form of BTC 3% stock redeemable between 1978 and 1988 and issued on 18 May 1948. In 1949, the directors were paid £50 between them for their expenses incurred in the company's dissolution. As managing director, and the receiver and manager of the Kent & East Sussex Light Railway and general manager and engineer of the East Kent Light Railway, Austen was given six months' notice to retire on 30 June 1949 with an *ex gratia* payment of £400; he had completed 40 years of railway service. His SMLR salary had been £525; the KESLR had paid him £500, and the EKLR £650 as well. R. F. Bowmaker, the part-time accountant was given three months' notice. On 20 December 1949 an assistant secretary of the BoT certified that there was no reason for the continued existence of the SMLR company.

Now completely under military control, the SMLR continued to provide a civilian service, running one train a day except on Sundays. BR personnel, presumably ex-SMLR employees in some cases, provided the public interface. In 1950 a loop line at Llanymynech was let to the North Wales Wagon Co Ltd to use for breaking up old wagons. There are no surviving records of the traffic carried during this period but the file dealing with the closure reveals that 2,258 tons of freight was carried in 1958. The three ex-LNWR coal tanks were sent to Swindon for scrapping in 1950 and the travelling crane followed them in 1953. The Royal Engineers took a fancy to *Gazelle*, though, and in 1950 arranged with the BTC for it to be loaned to them and put it on display at their Longmoor depot.

During the 1950s the railway was quite welcoming to enthusiasts, a letter seeking permission to ride on the goods train being met with a permit to show the train crews. In return, the visitors were expected to visit the operating officer in his Kinnerley office for a chat. After one group asked for permission

Above: **A staff train approaches Meole Brace with ex-LNWR 0-6-0 No 8182 in charge, in June 1947. The two clerestory vehicles are of GWR origin.**
Michael Whitehouse collection

Left: **The ex-LNWR coal engines were sent to Swindon for scrapping in 1950 and met their end there in November. On 24 September they were seen in the dump during an enthusiast visit, Nos 8182 and 8236 hiding behind No 8108.**
Author's collection

Above: **A visit to the SMLR by the Manchester Locomotive Society took place on 22 May 1955. At Criggion the party was taken to the quarry before posing for a photograph. The British Quarrying Company's Sentinel is stabled to the left.** *H. D. Bowtell/ A. M. Davies collection*

Right: **The Birmingham Locomotive Club special at Kinnerley on 26 June 1955. The railcars were set to ferry the party to Criggion.** *V. J. Bradley*

to walk from Kinnerley to Llanymynech, which was rarely used at that time, they were given the services of a railcar and driver for an impromptu railtour to the Melverley bridge and then to Llanymynech. The Birmingham Locomotive Club reprised its 1939 visit in June 1955 and the Stephenson Locomotive Society made the first of two visits on 21 September 1958.

Decisions made by the WD in 1957, not to retain the sub-depot at Ford and to close the Central Armaments Depot at Nesscliffe by 1960, brought with them the axiomatic conclusion that the railway should be closed and handed back to civilian control.

The BTC soon decided that the railway had no future and calculated that it would save £5,818 annually by not operating it. A formal closure application was submitted to the Transport Users Consultative Committee in July 1959. Because the WO 11,000v power supply was conveniently routed via Hookagate, BR decided that the site was suitable to establish a rail-welding depot, and had taken it over on 1 January 1959. Ford depot was closed on 1 September 1959.

The first stages in the dismemberment and dismantling of the SMLR came on 4 January 1960, with the closure of the Criggion branch, the last of the stone trains having run during December. On 26 February 1960 the main line was broken at Hookagate and west of Shrewsbury station: the former in connection with the welding depot construction, the latter to facilitate the construction of a spur to the Severn Valley line. Completed on 11 March, the spur made it possible for the Esso oil depot alongside the station to continue in operation. Although the remainder of the SMLR was closed with effect from 29 February 1960 an excursion over the railway, excluding the Abbey branch, was run for the Stephenson Locomotive Society on 20 March.

Much of the correspondence between the WD and the BTC concerning the SMLR had been conducted by Major Alan N. Stacey MBE of the Royal Engineers and John L. Bullock of BTC's commercial office. On 26 February 1960, Bullock wrote to Stacey: 'The Shropshire & Montgomeryshire Light Railway

has been fighting a valiant but losing battle for many years, and although the scars of the early occupation were partly healed by the present occupiers, this last engagement was decisive and it is sad to think that its demise will be without medals.'

Recovered military materials were worked via Llanymynech over the next few weeks and the SMLR was formally released to the BTC on 30 April 1960, leaving just a few administrative chores to complete. The WD and the BTC had to work their way through the 1941 inventory and account for anything that was missing or improved. A permanent way trolley valued at £600 was missing, the replacement of the original 70lb double-

Top: **WD No 141 at Hookagate with the civilian goods train on 25 June 1955. Notice the spark arrester on the chimney.** *V. J. Bradley*

Above: **Looking westwards at the War Department sidings at Hookagate on 26 June 1955.** *V. J. Bradley*

head rail with 75lb flat-bottom rail was assessed to be a £500 per mile improvement, and in the stores were found identifiable parts from locomotives long since scrapped, namely *Severn*, *Pyramus* and *Morous*. On 25 November 1964 the WD received a cheque from British Railways, London Midland Region for £7,550 in respect of the recovery of sidings and signalling at Llanymynech. There must have been other unfiled transactions.

As a light railway the SMLR had open level crossings at Pentre and Shoot Hill. Because the traffic was so heavy during the war, barriers had been installed. Noticing that the barriers had been removed, Shropshire County Council changed the road signs and invoiced the WD £32 0s 10d for doing so.

These were just a few fragments of railway remaining. Blodwell Junction had been closed to passengers previously, on 15 January 1951; with the TVLR truncated to Llanrhaiadr Mochnant from 1 July 1952 it was closed to freight on 6 January 1964. The southern end of the Nantmawr branch closed with the Llanfyllin branch on 18 January 1965. Nantmawr had been closed to public traffic on 6 January 1964 and although the stone traffic ceased on 21 October 1971 the track remained *in situ*, part near Blodwell Junction being used to aid shunting in Llanddu quarry until 1988. In 2004 the Oswestry-based Cambrian Railways Society announced that it had purchased the last remnant of the PSNWR to retain its rails, 1½ miles to Nantmawr quarry sidings from Llanddu Junction. In June 2006 the Office of Rail Regulation approved of the disposal of the TVLR/Cambrian branch to Gobowen by Network Rail to Shropshire County Council, finally isolating Nantmawr from the national network 140 years after the branch's construction.

The owners of Criggion quarries, the British Quarry Company, had leased Nantmawr from 1974 and closed it in 1977. The incline had been taken out of use in the 1950s and the

track covered in stone and a thin layer of tarmac enabling use by dumpers. Rails can still be seen where the surface has broken. The quarry, now owned by Hanson Aggregates, is used for leisure activities but in 2006 Hanson said that it had planning consent to resume quarrying although the quarry is dormant under the terms of the Environment Act 1995. Criggion, also owned by Hanson, is still in production, its output transported by road.

From 1963 until c1975 the Welsh Highland Light Railway (1964) Ltd established a base at Kinnerley station on which it stored various locomotives until it secured its site in Porthmadog. The Hookagate rail welding depot was closed in 1986. At Shrewsbury, the public goods service was withdrawn on 7 October 1968, the oil depot closed on 15 July 1988 and the track lifted in 1990 when the site became a car park. After a campaign to prevent their demolition, the station buildings were leased by the Shrewsbury Railway Heritage Trust in 2004 and a small museum may be established there when they have been restored. A new road near the station is named Old Potts Way and a section of the A5112 on Bage Way occupies a part of the PSNWR loop line trackbed.

Despite the closure of the ammunition depots the Ministry of Defence still has a presence in several locations in the area, around Pentre and Shrawardine in particular. At Pentre the trackbed has been made into an access road. Aerial photographs accessible on the internet reveal the classic ammunition store dispersal pattern near Kinnerley. For those armed with a good map there are still traces of the old railway to be found, notably some of France's bridges, although only the abutments of his grandest structure, the Shrawardine river bridge, survive. The northernmost abutment, with the old trackbed leading to it now a public footpath, serves as a viewing platform, complete with a thoughtfully provided bench. The Melverley river bridge was adapted to take road traffic in 1962, but the distinctive brick-built multi-arched bridge across the railway at Melverley station has gone. In parts, the trackbed has been ploughed out of existence; in others a corridor of overgrown scrub and unkempt trees delineate it.

Below: **Kinnerley depot under military control with two WD 0-6-0 STs on shed, 29 December 1955.**
F. W. Marshall/Alan Donaldson collection

Above: **The Stephenson Locomotive Society ran a railtour over the SMLR on 21 September 1958, seen with WD 0-6-0ST No 188 during a break at Kinnerley.** *R. F. Roberts*

Below: **On the same occasion No 189 was stopped for photographs on Shrawardine Viaduct.** *A. M. Davies*

Shropshire & Montgomeryshire Rly.
STEPHENSON LOCOMOTIVE SOCIETY
(MIDLAND AREA)
SPECIAL TRAIN TOUR
21st September, 1958
Shrewsbury (The Abbey), Kinnerley,
Llanymynech and return, also
Kinnerley-Criggion Branch.
Second Class.   Fare 10/-
Conditions as per itinerary.
030   030

Above: **Melverley bridge as rebuilt, seen on 10 October 1959, the occasion of an** *ad hoc* **railtour that took place in heavy rain.** *J. Peden / V. J. Bradley collection*

Right: **The BTC closure notice dated January 1960, posted on an SMLR notice board.** *A. M. Davies collection*

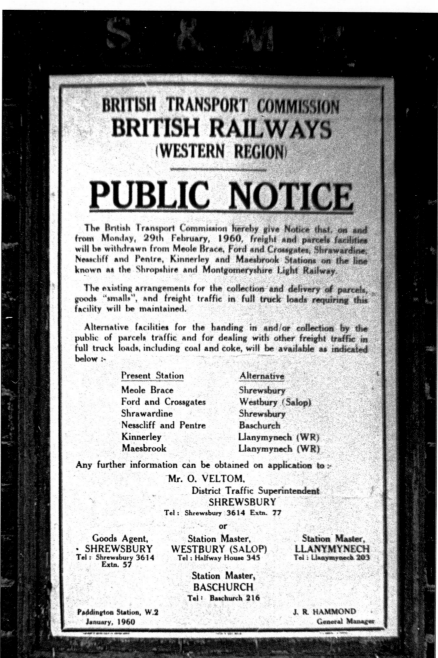

BRITISH TRANSPORT COMMISSION
BRITISH RAILWAYS
(WESTERN REGION)

PUBLIC NOTICE

The British Transport Commission hereby give Notice that, on and from Monday, 29th February, 1960, freight and parcels facilities will be withdrawn from Meole Brace, Ford and Crossgates, Shrawardine, Nesscliff and Pentre, Kinnerley and Maesbrook Stations on the line known as the Shropshire and Montgomeryshire Light Railway.

The existing arrangements for the collection and delivery of parcels, goods "smalls", and freight traffic in full truck loads requiring this facility will be maintained.

Alternative facilities for the handing in and/or collection by the public of parcels traffic and for dealing with other freight traffic in full truck loads, including coal and coke, will be available as indicated below :-

Present Station	Alternative
Meole Brace	Shrewsbury
Ford and Crossgates	Westbury (Salop)
Shrawardine	Shrewsbury
Nesscliff and Pentre	Baschurch
Kinnerley	Llanymynech (WR)
Maesbrook	Llanymynech (WR)

Any further information can be obtained on application to :-

Mr. O. VELTOM,
District Traffic Superintendent
SHREWSBURY
Tel : Shrewsbury 3614 Extn. 77

or

Goods Agent,	Station Master,	Station Master,
SHREWSBURY	WESTBURY (SALOP)	LLANYMYNECH
Tel : Shrewsbury 3614 Extn. 57	Tel : Halfway House 345	Tel : Llanymynech 203

Station Master,
BASCHURCH
Tel : Baschurch 216

Paddington Station, W.2
January, 1960

J. R. HAMMOND
General Manager

Top: **A photo stop on Shrawardine Viaduct must have been almost mandatory for enthusiast tours by this time. This was taken on 18 March, when most of the structure's original ironwork had been removed and replaced as required.** *Hugh Ballantyne*

Above: **The scene as viewed from the river bank. In the 21st century safety environment such occurrences could not be considered.** *A. M. Davies*

Left: **A steam crane was used for the demolition; seen in Nesscliffe depot, 1960.** *A. M. Davies*

Above: **Enthusiasts watch as WD 0-6-0ST Nos 188 and 193 are serviced at Kinnerley on 18 March 1960, during the final railtour.** *Hugh Ballantyne*

Right: **Nesscliffe depot with rails removed and sleepers still** *in situ*, **1960.** *A. M. Davies*

Below: **A view from the road bridge at Kinnerley after the track had been removed.** *Author's collection*

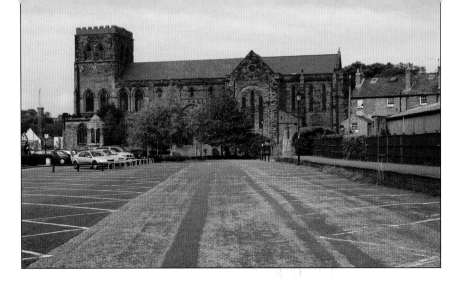

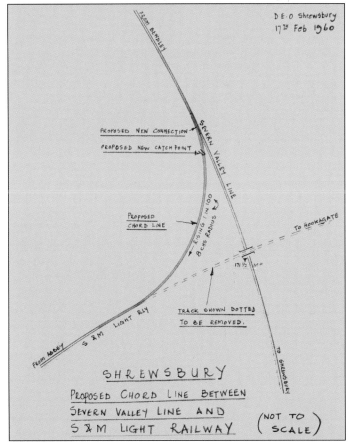

Above: **Shrewsbury station site, 7 October 2007. The refectory pulpit stands out above the cars; the station building is hidden by the hedge to the right of centre.** *Author*

Left: **A sketch of the chord connecting the Severn Valley line to the SMLR fragment at Shrewsbury.** *National Archives*

Bottom: **The site of Shrawardine Viaduct, looking west on 31 July 2007.**

Above: **One of France's double-track road bridges, Llwyntidmon Mill, near Maesbrook, 9 September 2007.** *Author*

Right: **Llanymynech station site cleared in advance of development, 9 September 2007.** *Author*

Below: **Built in 1947, Melverley bridge was adapted for road traffic in 1962; 7 October 2007.** *Author*

Above: **At Lane Farm, near the Criggion terminus, the trackbed is dominated by Breidden Hill; 7 October 2007.** *Author*

Left: **The maker's mark on an iron beam on the Nantmawr incline road bridge; 9 September 2007.** *Author*

Below: **Nantmawr branch terminus, looking west, 9 September 2007. The incline was out of sight to the right compare with photograph on page 59.** *Author*

Appendix 1
Locomotives and rolling stock

R. S. France

Manning, Wardle (140 of 1864) 0-6-0ST *Alyn*	To Mawddwy Railway contract
Manning, Wardle (151 of 1865) 0-6-0T *Powis*	To PSNWR
Manning, Wardle (167 of 1865) 0-6-0T *Sir Watkin*	To PSNWR
Manning, Wardle (168 of 1865) 0-6-0T *Viscount*	To PSNWR

Potteries, Shrewsbury & North Wales Railway

Manning, Wardle (151 of 1865) 0-6-0T *Powis*	From France 1866, sold 1888
Manning, Wardle (167 of 1865) 0-6-0T *Sir Watkin*	From France 1866, sold *c*1873
Manning, Wardle (168 of 1865) 0-6-0T *Bradford*	From France 1866, formerly *Viscount,* sold 1888
Bury, Curtis & Kennedy (1847) 0-4-2	LNWR No 1859, acquired 1872, scrapped by 1875
T. W. Worsdell (1863) 0-4-2T *Tanat*	Sold 1888
Yorkshire Engine Co (185 of 1872) 2-4-0T *Hope*	New to PSNWR, to East & West Junction Railway, 1888
Hawthorns Co (1865) 0-4-0WT *Breidden*	New to PSNWR, to Walker Brothers (Wigan) Ltd, 1873
Hughes (1864) 0-4-0ST *Nantmawr*	To Walker Brothers (Wigan) Ltd, 1873

There were four other locomotives, three disposed of in 1866 and one in 1872.

Hope was hired from the London Finance Association and Brown, Shipley & Co.

Charles Chambers

Manning, Wardle (1037 of 1887) 0-4-0ST *Wye*	Delivered to Chambers when working on Golden Valley Railway contract, left unused at Shrewsbury for SR work stopped. At Redheugh Colliery, Gateshead, *c*1891.

Shropshire & Montgomeryshire Light Railway

1	Dodman (1893) 0-4-2WT *Gazelle*	Acquired from Thomas Ward & Co, then rebuilt from 2-2-2WT in 1911, after a period out of use from early 1930s returned to service in 1937. Taken over by the War Department in 1941 and by British Railways in 1948. Transferred to the WD on loan, 1950.
2	Bury, Curtis & Kennedy (1853) 0-4-2ST *Hecate*	New to St Helens Railway, sold by LNWR to Griff Colliery, Nuneaton, *c*1870, named *Crewe*. Acquired 1911, renamed *Severn* in 1916 and scrapped April 1937, probably out of use since 1932.
3	Beyer, Peacock (1517 of 1875) 0-6-0 *Hesperus*	London & South Western Railway No 0324, acquired 1911 following overhaul at Eastleigh Works; livery dark green with light green lining. Allegedly reboiled in 1928. In 1937/8 only worked on Mondays, 'when the stone traffic is light'; 'a grand old engine'. Laid aside when seen by WO personnel in October 1940. Taken over by the War Department in 1941, probably scrapped October 1941.
4	Manning, Wardle (178 of 1866) 0-6-0ST *Morous*	Stratford & Midland Junction Railway No 1, acquired 1910, hired to the West Sussex Railway (Selsey Tramway), 1924, sold to WSR for £50 in 1932.
5	Hawthorn, Leslie (2878 of 1911) 0-6-2T *Pyramus*	New to SMLR, to War Department, Woolmer Military Instruction Railway, *c*1916.
6	Hawthorn, Leslie (2879 of 1911) 0-6-2T *Thisbe*	New to SMLR, to War Department, Woolmer Military Instruction Railway, *c*1916.
	Hudswell, Clarke (2459 of 1881) 0-6-0ST *Walton Park*	Weston, Clevedon & Portishead Light Railway No 4, acquired 1913 but sent to East Kent Railway, 28 April 1913; not numbered.
5 (2)	Beyer, Peacock (1428 of 1874) 0-6-0 *Pyramus*	London & South Western Railway No 0300, acquired 1914, withdrawn 1928, scrapped 1931, boiler fitted to No 6 (2).

6 (2)	Beyer, Peacock (1209 of 1873) 0-6-0 *Thisbe*	London & South Western Railway No 0283, acquired 1916, cost £745. Out of service 1935, sold for scrap 1937, £136.
7	London, Brighton & South Coast Railway (Brighton 1880) 0-6-0T *Hecate*	London, Brighton & South Coast Railway No 681 *Beulah*, acquired from the Admiralty at Invergordon, 1921, reported to be still in LBSCR livery in 1923. Withdrawn 1930, scrapped 1931, parts reused in other locomotives.
8	London, Brighton & South Coast Railway (Brighton 1878) 0-6-0T *Dido*	London, Brighton & South Coast Railway No 638 *Millwall*, acquired from War Stores Disposals Board, 1923, withdrawn 1930, scrapped 1934, parts reused in other locomotives.
9	London, Brighton & South Coast Railway (Brighton 1880) 0-6-0T *Daphne*	London, Brighton & South Coast Railway No 683 *Earlswood*, acquired from War Stores Disposals Board, 1923, apparently withdrawn 1931 but reported in an unidentified railway magazine to be still in service in 1933, to Southern Railway, Eastleigh, for spares.
8108/2 (2)	London & North Western Railway (Crewe 1869 of 1874) 0-6-0	London, Midland & Scottish Railway No 8108, acquired 1930, seen 'in store' in May 1937, retubed 1938. Overhauled at Crewe in 1941 and No 8108 restored. Taken into British Railways stock in 1948. Withdrawn by 1948, scrapped at Swindon 1950.
8182	London & North Western Railway (Crewe 2333 of 1879) 0-6-0	London, Midland & Scottish Railway No 8182, acquired 1931, taken into British Railways stock in 1948. Withdrawn by 1948, scrapped at Swindon 1950.
8236	London & North Western Railway (Crewe 2459 of 1881) 0-6-0	London, Midland & Scottish Railway No 8236, purchased 21 June 1932, taken into British Railways stock in 1948. Withdrawn by 1948, scrapped at Swindon 1950.

An 0-6-0T of Manning, Wardle appearance was used during the reconstruction; it might have been an early (*c*1866) Hunslet.

War Department
In addition to the five locomotives taken over from the SMLR some 50 steam locomotives and seven four-wheeled diesel locomotives were allocated to the SMLR by the WD for various periods between 1941 and 1960. Predominant initially were 15 GWR 'Dean' 0-6-0s; from 1944 the WD 'Austerity' 0-6-0Ts became ubiquitous. Three USA-built Porter 0-6-0STs were transferred during 1944 but were scrapped the following year. There were also 17 petrol trolleys used on the SMLR.

Railmotors
● Three-car passenger set built by Edmonds of Thetford with Ford engines in 1923. The centre car was taken out of use shortly after the set entered service and was transferred to the West Sussex Railway in 1931. The power cars were out of use from 1937 and sold for scrap 1943.
● A single railmotor built by Wolseley-Siddeley for the WSR in 1923, acquired *c*1928, may not have been used; certainly out of use by 1934.
● A Ford lorry with rail wheels was also obtained from the WSR with the Wolseley railmotor. It sometimes worked with one of the Edmonds railmotors, *c*1928 until 1930s.

Left: Four ex-GWR 0-6-0s, otherwise known as 'Dean Goods' on shed at Kinnerley in 1946. *Michael Whitehouse collection*

Appendix 2

Rolling stock survey
by War Office personnel,
October 1940

Goods Stock

Quantity	Type	Comment
1	5 ton-hand travelling train	New jib required
14	Open wagons, low sided, 8 tons	Bodies in poor condition, wheels and frames in fair order
9	Covered goods wagons	Wheels and frames in fair order, bodies developing defects, now being used as stores vans
7	Cattle wagons	In poor condition, now being used as stores vans
6	Bolster wagons	In fair order
2	Brake vans	One in use, the other under repair
1	Stores van	In poor condition

The stock generally is in poor condition but could be made serviceable within the depot.

Coaching stock

Quantity	Type	Comment
2	4-wheel	Ex-North Staffordshire Railway
4	4-wheel	Ex-Midland Railway
3	8-wheel	Ex-Caledonian Railway

The coaching stock is in a very bad state of repair. Some of the coaches could be cleaned up for military use on the line but would require new roofing canvas. Subject to the roofs being repaired and interiors removed other [sic] coaches could be used in the depot for temporary offices.

Appendix 3

Capital of the Potteries,
Shrewsbury & North Wales Railway and
the Shropshire Railways

	Capital authorised			Capital created or sanctioned		
	Stocks and shares £	Loans £	Total £	Stocks and shares £	Loans £	Total £
1862 Act	90,000	30,000	120,000	90,000	30,000	120,000
1863 Act	60,000	19,990	79,990	60,000	19,990	79,990
1864 New lines Act	200,000	66,000	266,000	200,000	66,000	266,000
1864 Branches Act	100,000	33,000	133,000	100,000	33,000	133,000
1865 North Wales Act	100,000	33,000	133,000	100,000	33,000	133,000
1865 Potteries Act	400,000	133,000	533,000	248,200	133,000	381,200
B Debentures					314,990	
A Debentures		70,000	70,000		70,000	70,000
1868 Scheme of arrangement between the company and creditors at the Chancery Court - issued in settlement of debt. (Debentures classified B)	60,000	19,800	79,800	60,000	19,800	79,800
C Debentures		135,000	135,000		135,000	135,000
1874 Act	50,000	16,600	66,600			
1888 Act			400,000			400,000
1891 Act	75,000	25,000	100,000		16,600	100,000
	908,200	581,390	1,963,600	858,200	556,390	1,897,000

Appendix 7

Shropshire Railways estimate of expenses,
1888 act

Railway No 1	3f 4½ch	Double
Gauge	4ft 8½in	£ s d
Embankments, including roads – 6,000cu yd		3,500 0 0
Retaining walls		3,600 0 0
Culverts and drains		1,000 0 0
Permanent way, including fencing: cost per mile: 3f 4½ch @ £4,100		1,768 2 6
Permanent way for sidings and cost of junctions		4,000
Stations		8,000
Contingencies at 10%		2,186 17 6
Total for construction of railway No 1		24,055 0 0
Land and buildings 4a 0r 0p		
Total cost of construction and of acquisition of land and buildings		24,055 0 0

Railway No 2	2f 2½ch	Double
Gauge	4ft 8½in	£ s d
Embankments, including roads – 4,000cu yd		2,333 6 8
Accommodation bridges and works		125 0 0
Culverts and drains		570 0 0
Permanent way, including fencing: cost per mile: 2f 2½ch @ £4,100		1,153 2 6
Permanent way for sidings and cost of junctions		1,000 0 0
Contingencies at 10%		518 10 10
Total for construction of railway No 1		5,700 0 0
Land and buildings 2a 1r 0p		500 0 0
Total cost of construction and of acquisition of land and buildings		6,200 0 0

Railway No 3				13 miles	Double
Gauge				4ft 8½in	
Construction of line	cu yd	Price/yd	£ s d		£ s d
Earthworks					
Cuttings – soft soil	420,000	1s 2d	24,500 0 0		
Roads	1,100	1s 6d	82 10 0		
Total	421,100		24,582 10 0		24,582 10 0
Embankments, including roads – 400,000cu yd					
Bridges – public roads – 14					9,200 0 0
Accommodation bridges and works					7,800 0 0
Viaducts					11,250 0 0
Culverts and drains including river bridge					3,300 0 0
Metalling of roads					1,130 0 0
Permanent way, including fencing:					
cost per mile: 13 miles @ £4,100					53,300 0 0
Permanent way for sidings and cost of junctions					8,000 0 0
Stations					6,000 0 0
Contingencies at 10%					12,456 10 0
Total for construction of railway No 3					137,019 0 0
Land and buildings 123a 0r 0p					18,450 0 0
Total cost of construction and of acquisition of land and buildings					155,469 0 0

Railway No 4				7 miles 2½ch	Double
Gauge				4ft 8½in	
Construction of line	cu yd	Price/yd	£ s d		£ s d
Earthworks					
Cuttings soft soil	330,000	1s 2d	19,250 0 0		
Roads	1,400	1s 6d	105 0 0		
Total	331,400		19,355 0 0		19,355 0 0
Embankments, including roads – 231,000cu yd					
Bridges – public roads – 12					7,600 0 0
Accommodation bridges and works					1,050 0 0
Culverts and drains					2,800 0 0
Metalling of roads					660 0 0
Permanent way, including fencing: cost per mile: 7 miles 2½ch @ £4,100					28,828 2 6
Permanent way for sidings and cost of junctions					5,000 0 0
Stations					4,000 0 0
Contingencies at 10%					6,929 17 6
Total for construction of railway No 4					76,223 0 0
Land and buildings 70a 0r 0p					7,000 0 0
Total cost of construction and of acquisition of land and buildings					83,223 0 0

Appendix 8

Shropshire Railways estimate of expenses, 1891 act

Railway No 1				4f 3ch	Single
Gauge				4ft 8½in	
Construction of line	cu yd	Price/yd	£ s d		£ s d
Earthworks					
Cuttings – soft soil	27,000	1s 2d	1,575 0 0		
Total			1,575 0 0		1,575 0 0
Accommodation bridges and works					250 0 0
Culverts and drains					100 0 0
Permanent way, including fencing:					
cost per mile: 4f 3ch @ £2,300					1,236 5 0
Permanent way for sidings and cost of junctions					1,200 0 0
Contingencies at 10%					436 15 0
Total for construction of railway No 1					4,798 0 0
Land and buildings 4a 0r 0p					800 0 0
Total cost of construction and of acquisition of land and buildings					5,598 0 0

Appendix 9

North Shropshire Light Railway (SMLR)
estimate of expenses

	£
Re-sleepering and relaying	7,800
Repairs and renewals to 40 bridges	1,250
Fencing	500
Repairs and renewals to all stations	3,950
Signalling and locking	900
Telephone	250
Allow for reconstructing Criggion branch	8,050
Equipment, rolling stock, engine shed and tools	6,100
Miscellaneous expenses	2,250
Light Railway Order, law etc.	750
Contingencies, say	2,450
Working capital	2,250
Financial fees, discounts etc.	3,500
	£40,000

Estimate of expenses for reconstructing the branch to Criggion

	£
Length of line 5 miles 10 chains	
Fencing, gates, and repairs to level crossings	1,841 5 0
Re-sleepering and relaying permanent way	3,309 9 7
Renewing Severn bridge and repairing one overbridge	1,289 5 5
Repairs and renewals to three stations	1,260 0 0
Signalling and locking	250 0 0
Telephone	100 0 0
	8,050 0 0

Appendix 10

Shropshire Light Railways
estimate of expenses

	cu yd	Price/yd	£ s d	£ s d
				£10 0s 0d
Preliminary Expenses				
Line No 1				2f 2½ch
Gauge				4ft 8½ch
Construction of line				
Earthworks				
Cuttings – rock				
soft soil	1,088	2s	108 16 0	
Total	**1,088**		**108 16 0**	**108 16 0**
Embankments, including roads – 8,176cu yd				
Bridges – public roads – none				
Accommodation bridges and works				50 0 0
Viaducts				
Culverts and drains				1,650 0 0
Metalling of roads and level crossings				
Gatekeepers houses at level crossings				
Permanent way, including fencing:				
cost per mile: 2f 2½ch @ £2,870				807 3 9
Permanent way for sidings and cost of junctions				1,000 0 0
Stations and buildings				
Plant, including signalling and telegraphic apparatus				120 0 0
Contingencies at 10%				373 0 3
Total for construction of line No 1				**4,109 0 0**

				£ s d
Land and buildings to be acquired for Line No 1				
2a 2r 0p				375 0 0
Total cost of construction and of acquisition of land and buildings				**4,484 0 0**
Rolling stock				120 0 0
General charges				20 0 0
Interest on capital during construction				807 0 0
Sundries				40 0 0
Total amount to be charged to capital				**5,481 0 0**

Preliminary Expenses				£490 0 0
Line No 2				21 m 7f
Gauge				4ft 8½in

Construction of line	cu yd	Price/yd	£ s d	£ s d
Earthworks				
Cuttings - rock	45,000	3s 6d	7,875 0 0	
soft soil	209,500	2s 0d	20,950 0 0	
roads	1,430	2s 6d	175 15 0	
Total	**255,930**		**29,003 15 0**	29,000 15 0
Embankments, including roads – 184,940cu yd				
Bridges – public roads – one				700 0 0
Accommodation bridges and works				2,500 0 0
Viaduct over River Severn				7,000 0 0
Culverts and drains				6,500 0 0
Metalling of roads and level crossings				625 0 0
Gatekeeper's houses at level crossings				
Permanent way, including fencing:				
cost per mile: 21m 7f @ £2,870				62,781 5 0
Permanent way for sidings and cost of junctions				6,000 0 0
Stations and buildings				5,000 0 0
Plant, including signalling and telegraphic apparatus				5,880 0 0
Contingencies at 10%				12,599 0 0
Total for construction of line No 2				**138,589 0 0**
Land and buildings to be acquired for Line No 2				
176a 0r 0p				17,600 0 0
Total cost of construction and of acquisition of land and buildings				**156,189 0 0**
Rolling stock				5,880 0 0
General charges				980 0 0
Interest on capital during construction				28,115 0 0
Sundries				1,960 0 0
Total amount to be charged to capital				**193,614 0 0**

Appendix 11

SMLR traffic and receipts
1913-1938

	1911	1912	1913	1914	1915	1916	1917	1918	1919	1920	1921	1922
Passenger traffic			64,976						68,156	74,702	67,166	52,289
Merchandise			5,841						5,514	4,299	2,014	1,992
Minerals			16,979						44,131	53,813	31,423	58,030
Coal			4,402						13		45	9
Tonnage			27,222						49,658	58,112	43,482	60,031
Livestock			8,556						3,965	3,371	3,721	2,087
Gross receipts			£4,593	£5,219	£6,998	£8,987	£11,438	£16,814	£16,737	£21,245	£23,426	£15,384
Expenditure			£3,649	£4,525	£6,110	£8,031	£10,374	£15,863	£14,078	£19,907	£21,760	£14,138
Net receipts			£944	£694	£888	£956	£1,064	£951	£2,659	£1,338	£1,666	£1,246

	1923	1924	1925	1926	1927	1928	1929	1930	1931	1932	1933	1934
Passenger traffic	49,730	45,571	38,182	27,821	22,102	19,719	16,555	13,637	11,352	9,116	3,248	604
Merchandise	2,305	2,685	1,824	1,607	1,083	1,040	1,345	694	641	845	692	520
Minerals	51,933	60,696	63,095	46,015	57,225	57,644	63,838	99,030	143,253	79,611	29,958	22,855
Coal	30	16		14	19	17	112			7	26	74
Tonnage	54,268	63,397	64,919	47,636	58,327	58,701	65,295	99,724	143,894	80,463	30,676	23,449
Livestock	2,938	6,235	4,731	4,086	3,197	999	1,720	1,605	959	579	523	129
Gross receipts	£15,074	£13,461	£13,471	£9,992	£11,252	£10,276	£10,416	£13,244	£16,499	£10,349	£5,334	£4,401
Expenditure	£13,443	£12,146	£12,279	£10,340	£9,942	£8,783	£9,009	£11,679	£14,839	£10,060	£6,150	£5,510
Net receipts	£1,631	£1,315	£1,192	-£348	£1,310	£1,493	£1,407	£1,565	£1,660	£289	-£816	-£1,109

	1935	1936	1937	1938
Passenger traffic	474	212	164	262
Merchandise	1,085	983	991	984
Minerals	41,853	23,969	20,533	16,931
Coal		19		
Tonnage	42,938	24,971	21,524	17,915
Livestock	297	269	32	66
Gross receipts	£6,642	£5,329	£4,950	£4,134
Expenditure	£6,173	£6,064	£6,361	£5,712
Net receipts	£469	-£735	-£1,411	-£1,578

SMLR traffic handled
1938–1940

Station	1938			1939			1940 (7 months)		
	Inwards tons	Outwards tons	Total	Inwards tons	Outwards tons	Total	Inwards tons	Outwards tons	Total
Abbey	13,782	92	13,874	15,580	68	15,648	7,360	53	7,413
Meole Brace	71	4	75	15		15	20		20
Hookagate	57	28	85	104	5	109	43	2	45
Edgebold	23		23	141		141	63		63
Cruckton	15		15	11		11		8	8
Ford & Crossgates	1,121	437	1,558	1,248	378	1,626	815	357	1,172
Shrawardine	62	13	75	59	616	675	74	311	385
Nesscliffe	629	9	638	849	10	859	451	13	464
Kinnerley	1,473	17	1,490	1,383	11	1,394	729	4	733
Maesbrook	345	6	351	346	2	348	255	5	260
Llanymynech	567	3	570	440	1	441	116	1	117
Criggion	929	13,785	14,714	549	10,005	10,554	18	360	378
Crew Green	78		78	17		17	20		20
Llandrinio Road	1		1		1	1			
Melverley	2	3	5	8		8	20		20
	19,155	14,397	33,552	20,750	11,097	31,847	9,984	1,114	11,098
Average daily tonnage			92			88			53

Appendix 13

SMLR approximate mileage and method of working
1940

Stations	Approx mileage between stations	Block working
Abbey		Staff & ticket
Meole Brace Junction	1½	
Meole Brace	½	
		Staff & ticket
Hookagate (Red Hill)	1	
Edgebold	1	
Cruckton	1	
Shoothill Halt	1¾	
Ford & Crossgates	¾	
		Tyers Electric Tablet No 7
Shrawardine	1¾	
Nesscliffe	2	
Kinnerley	2¼	
		Staff & ticket
Wernlas Halt	1½	
Maesbrook	1	
Llanymynech	2	
	18	

NOTES: Omnibus telephones at Shrewsbury, Meole Brace, Edgebold, Ford & Crossgates, Shrawardine, Nesscliffe, Kinnerley, Maesbrook and Llanymynech; block circuit between Ford & Crossgates and Kinnerley; Post Office telephone at Kinnerley.

Bibliography

Baughan, Peter; *A Regional History of the Railways of Great Britain Vol 11 North and Mid Wales*; David & Charles, 1980, 2nd Edition 1991

Carpenter, Roger; *The Criggion Branch of the Shropshire & Montgomeryshire Light Railway*; Wild Swan Publications, 1990

Carpenter, Roger; 'The colliers of the S&M'; *British Railway Journal*, No 18

Carpenter, Roger; 'The S&M Ford Railcar'; *British Railway Journal*, No 63

Carpenter, R. S.; 'Abbey Station of the Shropshire & Montgomeryshire Railway'; *British Railway Journal*, No 23

Garrett, Stephen & Scott-Morgan, John; *Colonel Stephens Railmotors*; Irwell Press, 1995

Industrial Locomotives of Cheshire, Shropshire & Herefordshire; Industrial Railway Society, 1977

Janes, Brian; 'The "Potteries" Railway and how it failed'; *Journal of the Railway & Canal Historical Society*, Nos 195/6, 2006

Lambert, A. P. & Woods, J.C; *Continent, Coalfield and Conservation – the biographical history of the British army austerity 0-6-0 saddle tank*; Industrial Railway Society, 1991

Lloyd, Mike; *The Tanat Valley Light Railway*; Wild Swan Publications, 1990

Mitchell, Vic & Smith, Keith; *Branch Line to Shrewsbury – The Shropshire & Montgomeryshire*; Middleton Press, 1991

Handbook to Shropshire & Montgomeryshire Railway; Shropshire & Montgomeryshire Light Railway Co, no date, *c*1920, reprinted Shropshire County Library, 1977

Peaty, Ian; *Moving Mountains by Rail – a history of quarry railways*; Tempus Publishing, 2006

Perkins, T. R.; 'A Derelict British Railway'; *The Railway Magazine*, May/June 1903

Perkins, T. R.; The Shropshire & Montgomeryshire Railway; *The Railway Magazine*, September 1911

Perkins, T. R. & Fox-Davies, F. E.; 'The Tanat Valley Light Railway'; *The Railway Magazine*, May 1904

Shaw, Philip & Mitchell, Vic; *Colonel Stephens – insights into the man and his empire*; Middleton Press, 2005

Shropshire & Montgomeryshire Light Railway Working Instructions; 1 Railway Group, Royal Engineers, 1956

Swift, P. H.; 'The LSWR Ilfracombe Goods 0-6-0s'; *British Railway Journal*, No 22

Taylor, James; 'Limited liability on trial: the commercial crisis of 1866 and its aftermath'; Paper presented to Economic History Society Conference, 2003

Tonks, Eric S.; *The Shropshire & Montgomeryshire Railway*; Author, 1949; 2nd edition, Industrial Railway Society, 1972

Turner, Keith & Susan; *The Shropshire & Montgomeryshire Light Railway*; David & Charles, 1982

Wren, Wilfrid J.; *The Tanat Valley – Its railways and industrial archaeology*; David & Charles, 1968

Wren, Wilfrid J.; *The Tanat Valley Light Railway*; Oakwood Press, 1979

Index

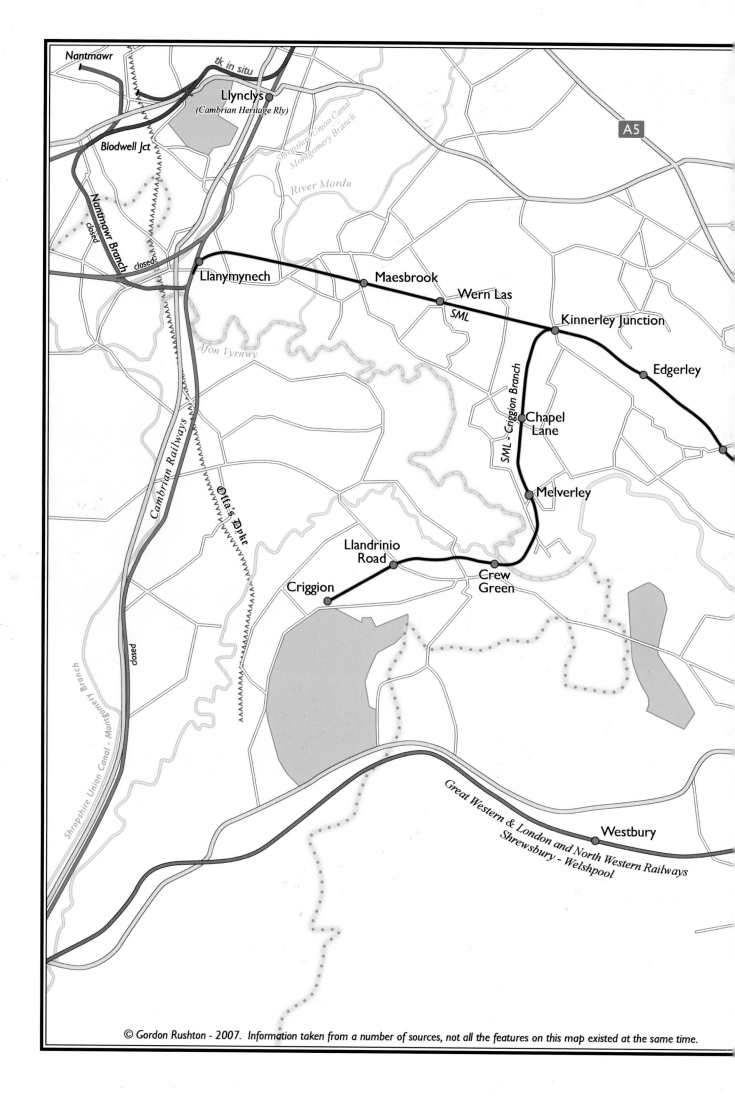

Nantmawr

tk in situ

Llynclys
(Cambrian Heritage Rly)

Blodwell Jct

Shropshire Union Canal
Montgomery Branch

River Mordu

A5

Nantmawr Branch

closed

closed

Llanymynech

Maesbrook

Wern Las

SML

Kinnerley Junction

Edgerley

Afon Vyrnwy

Cambrian Railways

Offa's Dyke

SML - Criggion Branch

Chapel Lane

Melverley

Llandrinio Road

Crew Green

Criggion

Shropshire Union Canal - Montgomery Branch

closed

Great Western & London and North Western Railways
Shrewsbury - Welshpool

Westbury

© Gordon Rushton - 2007. Information taken from a number of sources, not all the features on this map existed at the same time.